TRIBAL BRUNCH:

FOOD FOR HEALTH
AND FRIENDSHIP

KIRSTEN D'AGOSTARO SHOOK

For WWS, the little bird who flew away, and for Nana Mary, for always believing in my wacky ideas and encouraging me to be the weirdo I am, bright colors and all.

ABOUT THE AUTHOR

Kirsten is the owner of Black Cat Wellness, a personal training company inspiring and empowering people to be healthy, happy, and actively participating in their lives. She is the wife of a handsome electrician, the kitty momma to two beautiful cats, Bug and Evie "Little Stink," the mama to Little Turkey, and the daughter / sister / cousin / niece / granddaughter to an amazing family. She currently resides in Oak Park, CA, and runs a monthly brunch club, not surprisingly called Tribal Brunch. Email her at Tribal-Brunch@gmail.com

TABLE OF CONTENTS

RECIPES 43

FOREWORD

"Never trust a skinny cook."

I can't remember which well-padded chef said that, but I've always followed their advice. After all, if a cook's creations are that good, they'd be stuffing their own face with it. Am I right?

So, when I suggested Kirsten write a cookbook, my mouth wasn't anticipating we'd be trying her recipes. I just wanted her to be happy – to follow her passion – and to write off her expenses. I didn't want her to drag me with her. Kirsten is a beanpole. What's she going to have us eating? Kale? Quinoa? Or worse? Whatever it is, I know it'll be something my mouth's no-fat-no-flavor mantra will encourage us to run screaming from.

"Paula, I make a mean brownie." Okay, I humored her, trying hard to not torture my mouth with thoughts of a brownie whose butter didn't drizzle down my forearm. "Trust me, you'll love it."

As I not so eagerly anticipated the completion of *Tribal Brunch*, I steeled myself. No matter how unexcited my palate, I will drum up the necessary enthusiasm to support my friend in her efforts. No matter how healthy she tries to make me, I will show her that I still love her. No matter what green crap she encourages me to consume, I will smile and say, "Yummy!"

Orange, Mango, Carrot Goodness. Cauli-Hummus. Mexican Rice Style Quinoa. Yup, just as I thought – healthy…

Hello, what's this? Chicken Fried Steak! Pork Short Ribs! Bananas Foster!

B-b-b-but she's skinny!

Fig Bacon Burger? Eggplant Parmesan? Chicken and Dumplings?

My culinary reality has been shaken. My faith in the chefs whose body type I share has been shattered. My mouth is disappointed that I'm on the computer instead of in the kitchen.

Tribal Brunch is my new favorite cookbook. I love that the recipes are not only delicious, they're easy to prepare. They're perfect for my me-myself-and-I household (with yummy leftovers for lunch). And now I'm even eagerly anticipating the "ooos" and "aaahs" at my next dinner party.

Oh! And her brownie? It was absolutely phenomenal.

Paula D. Williams, EA

WHY DO YOU NEED TO READ THIS BOOK?

You've had a long day at work and can't wait to get home. You put your key in the door and open it to find the lights are dimmed, candles glow softly in the dining room, romantic music is playing in the background, and delicious aromas fill the air. "Oh yes," you think, "I'm being seduced!" But then you look down and see your belly protruding over your slacks. You panic, thinking, "I can't do this! He will expect me to be romantic. He will totally expect me to possibly get intimate after all of this. He will want me naked!"

The mere thought of jiggling flesh and soft body parts strikes fear in your heart. You are ashamed about your body. How could something so magical, something as wonderful as being romantic and intimate with your partner cause so much shame and guilt?

The next day, you might struggle with your decision. Should I have gotten naked or not? Should I have kept the lights on or off?

This type of internal dialogue leads to second guessing everything in your life. "I'm not pretty enough for that role," "Maybe I shouldn't try for that job because I'm too chubby," "Nobody likes me."

The shame you feel over your body impacts everything you do.

**Food affects how our body appears
and the appearance of our body
affects everything else in our lives.**

So let's take a look at the role of food and how we perceive food in the scheme of things.

That old saying, "You are what you eat," is pretty accurate. The fuel we put into our bodies directly affects how our bodies perform and look. Our bodies are machines and these intricate, complex systems thrive on proper nourishment. When we feed our systems cheeseburgers, French fries, and milkshakes, we are providing energy, but not clean, sustainable energy.

Imagine fueling our systems with high octane, robust, nutrient dense energy from proteins, fresh fruits, vegetables, healthy fats, and whole grains. This type of energy is cleaner, denser, and more sustainable. It allows our bodies to perform better. The burger and fries approach is like putting packing peanuts in the gas tank and expecting the car to run smoothly.

Providing our body with the fuel it requires allows it to function at its highest level. It gives the body energy so we can be the best version of ourselves that we can be. When we put packing peanuts in our tanks, we suffer the consequences of poor fuel intake. We can be groggy, our insulin levels flip out, and we aren't able to think clearly. We're not our best version of ourselves and can't make the best choices for our life. Our sleep is impacted. Our sex life is totally impacted. And for females, our cycles and hormones can be significantly impacted by poor nutrition causing us to experience problems with our thyroid, endocrine system, and even reproductive systems. In other words, poor nutrition makes all of our essential systems go completely out of whack!

Let's get back to that cheeseburger and fries. On occasion, a cheeseburger with fries is acceptable. The problem is, too many people eat this way regularly. The meat they choose is not always the best meat. It is the packing peanut version of meat.

You know what I'm talking about. Burgers at fast food restaurants are not made from high-quality beef. The cows that provide the meat are fattened up artificially, using growth hormones and even candy. Some farms in America actually feed their cows candy, still in the wrappers! That's how they cut the feed so the cows will fatten up.

So what happens when a cow eats candy? The same thing that happens to a human. The cow's sugar levels spike and their stress levels rise, producing high levels of hormones. Guess who eats those stress hormones? We do! We actually absorb the negative hormones in the meat.

Thich Nhat Hanh, a Vietnamese Buddhist monk, wrote about eating happy chickens. He said that when chickens are angry, they produce angry energy that is absorbed into their meat. The same thing happens with cows. The negative, angry, stressed energy that is in the hormones winds up in the meat we eat. So why eat scared, angry meat when you don't have to?

High-quality, high-grade beef, chicken, and fish will contain less harmful hormones and energy. I suggest looking for grass fed beef, from cows that are in pastures eating grass, not candy. These cows are loved, cared for, and raised naturally. The better the conditions, the better the well-being of the animal. This means less stress and fewer negative hormones in the food we eat.

Think of the difference between fast food beef, if that's what it even is, and Kobe beef. The same applies to chickens and fish. Chickens are often raised in such tight spaces that they fight constantly and have to be de-beaked. Farm raised fish are in very small, crowded ponds that breed sickness. This isn't only bad for the animals; it is bad for us. It's just plain bad. These animals are not living healthy lives. They are actually, for all intents and purposes, being abused just so we can eat them.

To avoid low quality products, look for grass-fed, pasture-raised beef, free-range organic chicken and fish. Start with the local farmers and get to know them. Find out who they are and what type of livestock or food they produce. Find out what you're eating by exploring your local area. Meet the farmers, meet the chickens, and meet the cows. Know what food you will be putting into your body and who is caring for that food before it comes to you.

Here are some key terms to look for and remember when you start investigating the food you eat:

Low Quality –
growth hormones, cut feed, additives, kennel raised, small
ponds

High Quality –
free range, natural, organic, pasture fed, grass fed

Now that you know what type of nourishment you should be purchasing, let's talk about eating it. Your body is a system, remember? That system needs to be fed a variety of foods in order to get everything it needs in the way of nutrients. This doesn't mean you have to eat every type of food at every meal, but you should be having enough variety in the course of a week to provide all the vitamins, minerals, and macro and micro nutrients your body requires to work at its best.

Chicken and Broccoli Every Night?

You'll be glad to hear that I definitely don't recommend eating the same thing every night. I don't even suggest you eat the same thing every other night. Too many times we focus on eating the same things over and over to ensure we are getting the proper balance of nutrients. In reality, we are depriving our bodies of specific nutrients that aren't always found in our core meals. Our systems don't only like variety, they need it!

An example of this would be if I had a steak with chard tonight. I would get a lot of protein from the steak and tons of nutrients from the chard. Tomorrow I might have more greens with some salmon and a sweet potato. This would give me a healthy dose of Omega 3 and Vitamin A. Don't look at nutrients as a daily checklist. Look at the whole picture.

Life happens and when the kids get sick or you have to work overtime and can't eat as planned, you want to know that there's room to play. Plan for the week or the month and have a general idea of what you will be fueling your body with, but don't be too rigid. This way, you know you've got a healthy array of foods at your disposal and you will be calmer when things don't go as planned.

There are also tons of options to eat well at restaurants. You can eat lettuce wrapped burgers and sweet potato fries instead of the traditional meal. Or just cut your portions in half. If wining and dining is something you really enjoy doing, why give that up? Absolutely keep that and just plan it out and see what you're eating the rest of the week so you keep things balanced. If you notice you ate too much or too little of one thing, remember to eat more vegetables or fewer grains with the next meal.

The goal is to avoid the really poor quality foods. Fast food burgers, again, are just really crappy options. In fact, there is a YouTube video floating around that shows a popular fast food burger soaked in hydrochloric acid, the same acid in the stomach. The burger doesn't even break down. Instead it turns into this disgusting black sludge. Another source reported that the bread at fast food restaurants is made with the same ingredient found in yoga mats. Yoga mats? That explains the elasticity, but it certainly isn't an ingredient I want in my body!

Energy In = Energy Out

Food is basically the energy we take in so we can put out energy. Our bodies burn a lot of energy on their own. They are amazing machines. They are constantly running. Think about it: our hearts pump every single moment, every single day of our entire lives, without ever stopping. We have neural activity that is constantly firing. There's actually electricity running through our bodies at all times.

Food is the gasoline that fuels our machines. It's what makes them run like beautiful performance cars. The better the gasoline, the better the car is going to run. When we have the right balance of energy in and energy out, the car not only performs better, it looks better because we are addressing the internal systems that keep it looking good on the outside. However, when that balance is off, the inside runs poorly and the outside shows it.

A negative energy system occurs when we take in fewer calories than our bodies need. We may exercise too much or eat too little. We will lose weight, but the weight we lose will result in a poor internal system that shows on the outside. Think of what starving people or prisoners of war look like.

They might be skinny, but they are not healthy. That is not where our bodies want to be. When we reach this point, non-essential functions shut down, like our endocrine and reproductive systems. Again, this poor nutrition can cause our brains to get sluggish, cause sleep problems, and lead to weak, poorly functioning systems. In other words, our bodies can't perform the way they are supposed to.

Then there's the positive energy balance. This is when we have too many calories coming in. That's where we are as a society. We haven't adjusted our caloric intake to our sedentary lifestyles. A lot of people sit at desks all day and still think that the need to eat 2000 calories to survive and that's just not factual.

Let's use the example of a weightlifter and a secretary. Both women have great, important jobs, but the weightlifter needs a lot more fuel in a day than the secretary. So the fuel they consume, the food they eat, will have to be different.

I'm Not Fat... I'm Skinny Fat – Is That Okay?

Skinny fat is the prisoner of war, the starvation victim. You might look skinny, but you could still be fat. If we starve our bodies of the nutrients it needs, our bodies lose weight, but also lose muscle tone. This means we can have a "normal" weight and a "high" body fat percentage.

Thin, in my opinion, is no longer beautiful. Fit and healthy is beautiful. The female figure comes from fat and muscle. When you work out, the muscles on the back of the rib cage, the latissimus dorsi muscle, develop a natural curve. It's the top of the hourglass figure. The three sections of the glutes have a beautiful curve, the waist — all of these muscle areas contribute to what we know as the female figure. When these areas are strong, they don't make us look manly, they make us look beautiful and strong, no matter what size we are.

Think of our ancestors. They didn't eat fast food or food injected with growth hormones, and they were beautifully strong. The women were gatherers. They carried weight, they walked for miles each day, and they foraged for food. They were bending down, squatting, standing, running, carrying children, baskets, weight bearing things. They were muscular and strong, but very shapely.

Another benefit of avoiding skinny fat is that with physical strength and muscle tone comes physical health. When we have strong bodies that support our machines, our systems run better in every aspect. This means that we can fight off infection and illnesses better when we are physically strong and our bodies are properly nourished, meaning less time and money spent at the doctor and more time and possibly money spent doing what we love with the ones we love. If we get sick, we have reserves that we can use to rebuild tissue and cells. When we're skinny fat, there's nothing to pull from, it's all fluff. It is imperative to pay attention to the percentage of body fat, or as health industry jargon refer to it, personal BFP.

Someone can have a high percentage of body fat at a low weight, such as 120 pounds with 35% body fat, or you can be at 160 pounds with 22% body fat, and that's a whole different thing. The person who weighs more might actually be a smaller size because muscle weighs more. The person with lower fat to muscle ratio will have more energy, burn more calories, sleep better, and have more sexual stamina. They will generally be a happier person because they are releasing endorphins and being more physically active throughout the day.

As women we are nurturers. We want to take care of everyone, especially our families, and make sure they're all set. As a result, we often put ourselves on the back burner, but the truth is, if we don't put on our oxygen mask first, we won't be able to help anyone else!

Consequently, when we are taking care of ourselves: exercising, eating healthy, meditating, nourishing our souls, we are also ensuring that we will be there for our families and loved ones in the long run, and we will be healthy, happy, and have ample energy for nurturing others!

Additionally, the benefit of women taking care of themselves is that we become amazing role models! By demonstrating the importance of a healthy lifestyle and taking time to ourselves, we are "giving permission" for others to take care of themselves, and to treat that as an important aspect of life without feeling guilty.

Pre-planning and effective time management are important components in this game. Treat exercise time as a "Very Important Appointment with Yourself."

Don't Break Your Appointment with Yourself!

I'm not saying to be selfish. You don't have to spend five hours a day working out. For some people that works, but unless you are a professional bikini model, that's not very realistic. Set aside time in your schedule that works for you, even if it is 30 minutes at 5AM, every other day.

One of my clients, let's call her Jane, told me that she had a job where she would leave early in the morning and get home by 8PM at night, so from 6AM to 8PM she had no time for herself! One day the light bulb went off, and she set an appointment with herself on Friday night. When people at work asked her to stay longer, she said, "I'm sorry I have an appointment."

Once she started doing that on Friday nights, she said to herself, "Hey wait, what if I booked some time on Tuesday's at lunch to do some exercising at the gym?"

You can create anything you want! You are just limited by your imagination, and we all know how limitless our imaginations are!

One of the problems that prevents women from taking care of themselves is the sense of "self-worth," we feel so guilty being good to ourselves and almost "not-worthy."

It's really sad and ridiculous at the same time. Women run the world – we raise the families, we run households, we work, and it's absolutely ridiculous that we feel guilty about getting our nails done. It is time to change that!

It doesn't take a whole lot of time to be strong and self-confident!

It can start right now, you just need to make a choice and stick to it!

Build Your Own Tribe

Modern women have strayed from the path of being strong and empowered. We have become super focused on our families and have been taking time away from ourselves and our female friends. Many of us have lost the community that women had in the past. Before the 50s, women lived in villages and had their communities, where everyone mattered and everyone had to raise each other's children. My kids were your kids and your kids were mine. However, during the fifties, women had to step up and build our own homes, raise our own children, and ultimately, that's how we lost our touch with the community.

We had forgotten how it feels to talk to other women and have that female support system. We each had our own little homes, cars, yards, and little family, but the support system that we had throughout time with our sisters essentially disappeared.

No wonder the fifties were the times when women started drinking and taking pills and really struggling from isolation. That sisterhood/support system was no longer there.

That support system is still missing in our society, especially with the growth of "social media addiction." As we become more and more connected "superficially," we become less connected on a deep, human level. Prince Ea has a great video called "Can We Auto-Correct Humanity?" on YouTube talking about this very thing. Check it out here:
https://youtu.be/dRl8EIhrQjQ.

We are trying to comfort ourselves through eating too many carbohydrates, or we're beating ourselves up and shaming our bodies because we see models who have been photoshopped into an unrealistic body type. If we don't look like that, we are failures.

My deep belief is that we need to foster that lost connection and be empowering for each other. I think many eating disorders originate because we do not have the sense of community and support for each other that women once shared.

An example would be having a pot luck with your female friends, where you have yummy, orgasmic food, and giggle about it and watch movies and drink wine. If it's appropriate, you bring your babies, young sisters, and your teenage daughters to cultivate that sense of community in them as well.

There are so many healthy fun foods, like foods that crunch, foods that are squishy, foods that are velvety, so just simply talking about the food and your experience of it can be a cause to get together!

Where Would I Start?

You could call a girlfriend and say, "Hey, come on over! Bring some chocolate or some wine. I'll cook a spaghetti dinner, and let's just laugh together, cry together, do 'nothing' together – let's get down to who we are and how we can support each other in our lives." I am positive that everybody has one girlfriend, co-worker, friendly neighbor, gym-mate that they can call up. There is someone! Just make the call!

It starts with one person. If you don't think you're special, you can be special in someone's life. Reach out, open your heart, open your door!

By reaching out to that person, you're really honoring the other person, saying what's actually not being said: "You're important, you're beautiful, and I want to spend time with you and contribute to you." That's going to make someone feel really awesome. That second person will probably call a third, and then so on and so on. All of a sudden, you have this community of women just talking and laughing and being together to encourage fortifying each other, building strength in one another, and seeing the beauty of each other, the inside making them gorgeous, and knowing that they're loved no matter what and it doesn't matter if there's a roll here or washboard abs. It doesn't matter -- it's just a community. It's a tribe.

I swear that I have only beautiful friends. In all of their shapes and sizes, these are gorgeous women who show me they can achieve anything and inspire me to do the things that scare me. I'd be crazy not to brunch with them monthly.

Kirsten's Journey

My eating disorder started when I was five years old, just as my parents were going through a divorce. For various reasons, my one-year-old brother and I were alone for long periods of time, so at five years old I had to feed the two of us. The only foods that I could make were hot dogs and scrambled eggs, which we did not always have in the fridge. When we would have food, we ate as much as we could so we wouldn't be hungry. That was really my safety, knowing that I could eat a lot and I wouldn't feel hungry. After a year, maybe even less, my parents got everything worked out and we were no longer left to fend for ourselves; however, I kept eating the same way. I had developed a feast or famine mentality.

When I got to high school and started playing volleyball, I became body conscious. I realized I was chubby, so I started not eating. This developed to the point that I got benched for anorexia. I had dropped a lot of weight. I was trying to be a high-performing athlete, so I went back to eating.

That same year, I broke my hip. The muscles pulled apart from my growth plate. I was really depressed and not eating again. Then I started eating to comfort myself, and once again, I spun out of control with my eating.

At 23, I had a boyfriend who was killed in a car accident. Once again, I stopped eating, as if this were somehow going to help deal with the depression.

This time my body was really rebelling. My sleep cycle was off, my hormones were off, my period actually stopped for nine months, my hair started falling out, my skin was very gray. I felt very lonely and very shameful.

When I realized my dead boyfriend would be really pissed off about me not eating and someone looked at me and said, "You look absolutely disgusting," I went back to binge eating, but I started to do it with nutrient dense foods. Instead of Cheetos it was kale chips, a salad, cashew nuts. You can be binge eat on anything! The issue of binge eating still remains, though. It's all about the headspace.

On the brighter side, my eating disorder was never completely crazy. I didn't eat out of trash cans. I didn't go to the grocery store and steal food. I didn't eat and vomit food. A lot of my sisters with eating disorders have done those things and have since sought out help. For me, it was just ruling my life. There was a time when I was sitting in my car with dark chocolate covered cashews, and I couldn't stop eating them. I remember thinking, "I really don't want to eat these. I want to just stop," and I couldn't. There's a great reenactment on the Black Cat Fitness YouTube page called Dark Chocolate Covered Cashews.

Apparently what was running the show that whole time was the scared five-year-old Kirsten saying, "You're unhappy, you're scared, you're anxious. You have all of these emotions that you're not really feeling, and you're trying to cover it and smother it with dark chocolate covered cashews and kale chips." You can also see the video about my younger self running my grownup body on YouTube.

Finally, I went through therapy in addition to support group meetings and all those things together brought me peace of mind and I realized that I don't have to be a scared five year old anymore.

My epiphany came when I was driving one day. In my mind's eye, I saw my five-year-old self, a tiny, helpless child, and finally realized how scared she was. All of a sudden my heart felt immense compassion for myself, and I said to her, "You must have been very scared, sweetheart. I'm sorry you went through that. It wasn't your fault, and you should know that."

Once I became clear on that, that it wasn't my fault, I realized that I don't have to eat like that anymore.

Of course, I still struggle with wanting to eat. While 2015 offered many new gifts, friendships, and exciting adventures, it also came with immense heartache. My husband's grandmother, Nana Mary, was killed in April by a house fire. It was terrible, horrendous, and pretty much the worst thing you can imagine. Through that next month, I was able to keep my eating under control and kept thinking about how she would be so pissed if I was making myself sick over her passing.

The following month, Warren, my husband, and I were blessed with pregnancy. What a happy, exciting time! How do I eat to maintain my health for myself and my little bird, as I called him? I reached out and started a community of women. In fact, that's my tribe on the cover of this very book. A couple of them even knew I was carrying Little Bird at the photoshoot for the cover.

July 7 is the day it all changed for the little Shook family. "What are you doing right now?" That's not a promising start with your ob/gyn when you're not close friends.

"I'm driving, so just tell me how bad it is." And she proceeded to tell me how sorry she was that I was losing my first baby.

What got me through? My family, my sisterhood, and my tribe. Despite not wanting to, I still led Tribal Brunch monthly gatherings. I asked myself what I was doing when I started to binge eat, and I found peace and comfort in that sisterhood. I was able to not go crazy with food because of all the love and support my community offered.

Eating Disorder Community

The eating disorder community specifically is very shameful and quiet. We're in the closet, and a lot of times we're just ashamed that we're eating, not eating, how we look, and how we feel. We are not alone, though. We can be empowered when we start to come out of our own head space and be around people who are going through the exact same thing and say, "Hey, I got your back. What's going on in your world?"

Binge eating can incorporate the anorexia. It's a cycle. Diets are the worst thing ever. I say that because the first three letters in the word "diet" are "die," which doesn't sound like something I want to do today.

Dieting is an unrealistic thing to do because the moment you're on the Atkins, Paleo, South Beach diet and you're eating to plan, there's someone's birthday or a life event happens, and you eat a piece of chocolate cake, and you've blown the whole thing. All of a sudden, you are feeling shitty, like you're fat, like you're ugly, like you can't stick to a plan, and it's just like, whoa! That's not self-loving! The diet plan sets you up for failure, and so then you go to the other extreme and you think, "I blew the diet, so I might as well just eat chocolate every day for the next 10 weeks, three times a day." Then you've yo-yo'd back to where you started, and you're ashamed of that.

Each time you yo-yo, it's harder to lose weight. You've done more internal damage. Finding a healthy eating lifestyle is going to help your guts, your body, your looks, and your self-esteem.

This book is all about lifestyle and not diets! We are not following Paleo or Atkins or South Beach – there's so many I can't keep track of them. These are just healthy, nourishing recipes for 21 days, which will help to jumpstart your new healthy lifestyle. The number 21 is not accidental, that's exactly how long it takes to break the old patterns and rewire your brain cells with new habits.

There's something for everyone in these recipes. For example, I can't eat wheat, but I still love spaghetti, so I am giving a squash spaghetti recipe or an almond flour pancake instead of regular one.

I don't want to diet. I want to celebrate life with food, which goes back to my Italian/Scottish heritage of family time. You celebrate with food! Any big thing, there's food!

It might sound scary and some of the foods will look new, but once you learn how to make them, they'll be super easy! Some recipes take only 20 minutes from beginning to end!

Get the Right Ingredients

On your journey to a healthy lifestyle, be sure to explore health-conscious grocery stores in your area. The Sprouts stores are really great in Southern California, close to where I live, where you can get a lot of the specialty items for people with lots of different intolerances. They've got a wonderful organic department and a great meat section.

While we're talking about markets, there is one really important tip to remember. The place to shop at a grocery store is the perimeter. The stuff in the aisles is junk you don't really need. The aisles are stocked primarily with processed foods. So remember the tribal people, they ate whole foods. If you need spices, go down the aisles while avoiding the cereals that are not good for your digestive tract. If you look at the labels and you can't pronounce what's in it, don't buy it. Just put it down and walk away calmly. Within the last 30 years, we've gotten all these weird foods, and we're totally not meant to eat them. That's why we have all these gluten intolerances and peanut and dairy allergies. Very few people are able to successfully digest dairy, and those who can generally overindulge. The central part of the store is not where we're meant to be. We're meant to be on the outside of it foraging for vegetables, fruits, nuts, and meat.

To avoid the processed foods, and to support the local farmers, you should also be shopping at your local farmer's market. At my local farmer's market, they have the usual vegetables and even a guy who sells grass-fed beef. There's a chicken and turkey vendor who has pasture raised chickens. The young kid who used to work there would say, "The ladies are super fresh today!" You've also got the fishmonger who was out catching the fish the day before. You can also find exquisite bakeries if bread and pastries are your thing. There are even people who sell healthy dog treats made out of pumpkin and other natural and delicious foods. There are all sorts of local support that you can give to the farmers at your local farmer's market, and working with fresh, real ingredients, you're setting your entire body up for better health.

HOW TO USE THIS BOOK

Recipe Details

The details in recipes are vital, especially for people who may not know how to cook as well as others. For example, this book contains a marinara sauce recipe. If I was to say, "Just throw in a pinch of this and smell it," which is what I do, it is not going to turn out the same for them. My pinch of it might not be the same as their pinch of it. Plus, you can't smell salt, so you wouldn't know how much more to add in because it is too basic of an instruction. But if I say you need one onion, two cans of this, or a teaspoon of salt, these measurements make it possible to confidently cook a meal. This is how someone gets comfortable while learning the basics of cooking. When they get more confident, then they can go on and add whatever they like their dishes. As such, I've done my best to provide instructions throughout to make it as painless as possible for you.

For those of you who may not cook as well as you would like, I urge you to read the entire recipe before you begin. This means reading the ingredients, the tools, the directions, and the notes. Everything. Maybe even two times through! Always take out all of your ingredients and tools, and have them ready on the counter. Because you may very well have ground meat all over your hands, this will greatly reduce the stress of trying to open cabinets and remove spices or get other ingredients as you go. Most importantly, just keep practicing your cooking skills! Like Dory from *Finding Nemo* says, "Just keep swimming!" Or cooking in this instance.

Snack Options?

Of course, you can't always be eating prepared meals. For snacks, I grab packs of nuts, a banana, apples with any kind of nut butter, cashew, almond, macadamia nut, celery with a nut butter, carrots, cucumber, hummus, that sort of stuff.

The reason I don't mention peanut butter is because peanuts are actually a bean. They're not a nut at all! Additionally, a lot of the processing that goes into peanuts and peanut butter is harmful. Peanuts are often raised in cotton fields, and the cotton is sprayed with lots of pesticides to keep the bugs away. Then peanuts are planted once the cotton is harvested. Peanuts help to sweeten the soil for the next batch of cotton. The peanuts are growing in this pesticide-infested earth and as they grow, they've got the pesticides in them. If you love peanut butter, I highly recommend going with an organic peanut butter.

While we're talking about nuts – eat them raw. I know it's delicious to have honey-roasted nuts, but the chemical property of nuts change when they're roasted. We don't get the full nutritional benefits from them if they're cooked. Also, you don't need a whole lot of them. Think just about the length and width of your own thumb.

Meal Plan

The lifestyle change and meal plan concept for me is to handle it week by week. It might be different for vegetarians, but it's the same concept. I like to give a different meat for each night of the week. Monday might be beef, Tuesday chicken, Wednesday fish, Thursday pork, and maybe Friday is the night I go out, so I don't plan anything. This brings us to Saturday, and I might say we haven't had steak, so let's have steak, and maybe Sunday is vegetarian. I personally really love having leftovers for lunch the next day, so it's perfect. Just put it in a container, store it in the refrigerator, and you don't have to worry about tomorrow's lunch. A great way to remember to take the lunch with you is go ahead and pack your lunch box, put it in the refrigerator, and leave your keys on it to make sure you take it with you. Generally we don't leave the house without them. Do the same thing at work.

If you don't have leftovers from dinner for next day lunch, you can simply make a quick and healthy salad. Thinking about the protein aspect of the lunch, you can throw in any kind of nuts to serve as protein. You can even use meat that you won't be using during dinner that night. Let's say you are making chicken for dinner, so make a tuna salad for lunch. This just makes it really simple.

If you are not home for lunch, keep nutrients in mind. Some people can budget to eat out, so if you can afford it, keep these three things in mind: protein, vegetables (not fruit), and a little bit of healthy fat. Healthy fats include avocados and olive and coconut oils. You want your food to be super colorful. When you sit there and look at your food, your brain starts to take in the nutrients and release the enzymes, which are sent throughout your body. Take your time and enjoy the meal. Perhaps take a moment to give gratitude to your food, whether it be out loud or in your head. Chew the meal fully so your body will know what to do with it. It's all about being mindful.

To elaborate on the idea of mindful eating, the process you take to eat and enjoy your meal is key because one must eat with their eyes first. By looking at the food and taking in the nutrients, it brings a good energy to the meal and how it enters your body. We like things that are pleasing, so when we are attracted to someone, we like to look at them. Looking at your meal is the same. When we admire the food, we bring on the good woowoo vibes and are being grateful for it coming into our bodies and going to our cells.

Think about this: if you are constantly sick, missing days of work, and are consistently going to the doctor, think about the food you are eating. I would venture to say that processed foods are the main component of your diet. What if you slowly adjusted to eating more whole foods, less processed foods, and a little bit of exercise? The medical bills will start to decrease, leaving you able to buy higher quality foods. Start with the "Dirty Dozen," the 12 most contaminated veggies and fruits from pesticides. They are apples, peaches, nectarines, strawberries, grapes, celery, spinach, bell peppers, cucumbers, tomatoes, snap peas, and potatoes. One easy way to keep track of what you should eat organic is to look at the skin. If it has thin skin, buy organic.

Another fun piece of information, eating healthier increases your sex drive, energy, and helps the joints. Take care of your immune system, digestive systems, and be healthy.

If you work on Sundays, don't do your meal planning that day. Figure out which days of the week work for you to spend a half hour to hour planning. The last thing you should do is make life and your health even harder for you to handle. That's not what we are about. Another thing that has made it easier for me while I am making my meal plans is asking my husband, "I need your help with food ideas." Don't feel bad about asking others what they would like to eat. They can help you come up with recipes and make the meal planning experience easier and more fun. My husband actually liked the idea of me asking him for ideas, and he went online and started sending me tons of recipes of things he thought sounded good. It became a fun game to play.

Another great idea is to lineup your cookbooks and mark up all the dishes you would like to try. Simply just go through it daily and prepare it for either that night or the next day's dinner. Change it up every week. If you have kids in the house, you can get them involved as well. Assign them weekdays and have them chose the dinner for that night of the week. Timmy gets to pick Tuesdays, your spouse gets Wednesday, and Fiona has Thursday. You can also set up recurring themes, like Taco Tuesdays or Meatless Mondays. At my dad's house when I was growing up, we had Friday Pizza and Movie Night. Part of the plan was that we would rent two movies from the video store (ahh... memories). Dad would make the pizza dough from scratch right before we started watching the first movie. We'd watch the first movie while the dough rose. The second movie was for the actual eating of pizza. My brother and I got to choose the different toppings, and it made us feel like what we had to say mattered.

What I would like to emphasis about meal plans is it's not what works for everyone, it's what works for you as an individual and/or family unit. Organization is key in meal plans, and as one my fantastic coaches says, "Plan your work and work your plan." When you have a plan, you have something to follow. You aren't running around in chaos. It comes more naturally with ease and grace, and it actually gives you the free time to do whatever is truly important to you, whether it's work, family time, or alone time.

Having a lot of time on your hands, since you don't have to worry about dinner every night, is what makes meal planning so great. What would it be like to actually have the time and energy to workout or just play with your kids? Pretty neat, huh?

This extra time actually gave me the idea to create a ladies brunch where we all come together and plan. You can have all the girls get together and share their own recipes. This is a great way to share and enjoy the company of other women while giggling and being healthy. It's as if you are bringing your family and coming together as one. This can even turn into a review session, and you can share which products work for you or how last night's dinner turned out. Just bring your tribe together. Call it Tribal Brunch if you want. Plan your work and work your plan!

Tools

There are some great tools out there that I would recommend to help make dinner faster.

- **Crock po**t – Put everything in, put the lid on, and turn the heat on!

- **Food processor** – This item is cool because it has attachments, like a shredding disk or slicer, making its uses extremely diverse!

- **Knives** – Having the right knives determines things like whether or not you will cry while cutting onions. A good knife will cut through the layers and it won't make you cry. You should learn to sharpen your own knives or find someone to sharpen your knives regularly. My knife sharpener actually goes to my farmers market each week.

Invest in good tools. This does not mean you have to buy the most expensive ones, just what feels good in your hands. Other great tools are pots and pans. These are the perfect tools to invest in. I recommend using plastic cutting boards for your meats so you can put them in the dishwasher. For your fruits and vegetables, I recommend the wooden cutting boards. Always keep them separate. Depending on my mood, I either purchase already chopped or whole vegetables from the market. If you are always on the go, then you can easily purchase the already chopped vegetables and fruits. Just be sure to rinse them at home.

21 DAY MEAL PLAN
(BECAUSE IT ONLY TAKES 21 DAYS TO CREATE NEW HABIT PATTERNS!) CREATE NEW HABITS TO CREATE A NEW YOU!

Week 1			
	Breakfast	**Lunch**	**Dinner**
Mon.	Cashew butter smoothie	Salmon w/lemon	Lemon Pepper Chicken Breasts Green Beans and Shallots
Tues.	Sweet potato hash	Leftovers	Broiled Steak Sautéed Spinach and Pine Nuts
Wed.	Berry smoothie	Leftovers	Fish Tacos Mexican Rice Style Quinoa
Thur.	Sweet potato hash	Leftovers	Spaghetti Squash and Meatballs Green Salad with Balsamic Dressing
Fri.	Cashew Butter Smoothie	Leftovers	Pork Short Ribs Mashed Plantains
Sat.	Almond Pancakes	Leftovers	Roast Chicken Green Salad with Balsamic Dressing
Sun.	Quiche	Leftovers	Salmon with Lemon Asparagus

Week 2			
	Breakfast	**Lunch**	**Dinner**
Mon.	Leftover Quiche	Rest of Leftovers	Chicken Fried Steak Mashed Cauliflower
Tues.	Cashew Butter Smoothie	Leftovers	Orange Trout Butternut Squash Soup
Wed.	Almond Pancakes	Leftovers	Zucchini Lasagna Beet Salad
Thurs.	Berry Smoothie	Leftovers	Barbecue Chicken Mashed Sweet Potatoes
Fri.	Sweet Potato Hash	Leftovers (except BBQ Chicken)	White Fish w/ Macadamia Nuts and Orange Asparagus
Sat.	Quiche	Leftovers (except BBQ Chicken)	Barbecue Pizza Green Salad with Balsamic Dressing
Sun.	Frittata	Leftovers	Stuffed Pasilla Peppers Cauliflower Rice (spiced with fresh cilantro)

Week 3			
	Breakfast	**Lunch**	**Dinner**
Mon.	Leftover Quiche or Frittata	Leftovers	Eggplant Parmesan Sautéed Swiss Chard
Tues.	Leftover Quiche or Frittata	Leftovers	Shrimp Curry Cauliflower Rice
Wed.	Leftover Quiche or Frittata	Leftovers	Pork Tenderloin
Thurs.	Cashew Butter Smoothie	Leftovers	Beef Moussaka Tomato and Cucumber Salad
Fri.	Berry Smoothie	Leftovers	Salmon with Lemon Roasted Radishes
Sat.	Almond Pancakes	Leftovers	Chicken and Dumplings Green Salad with Balsamic
Sun.	Sweet Potato Hash	Leftovers	Fig Bacon Burger Sauteed Brussels Sprouts

SHOPPING LIST

WEEK 1 SHOPPING LIST		
Produce	**Pantry**	**Meat**
3-4 bananas	4 cups almond flour	4 chicken breasts, boneless skinless
2 carrots	1 bottle BBQ Sauce	
1 bunch endive	1 can coconut milk	18 eggs
1 bunch fresh dill	14.5 oz canned diced tomatoes	1 lb. ground meat (optional)
1 bag frozen mixed berries	2 cans whole tomatoes	3-4 lb. pork short ribs
1-2 heads of garlic	16 oz. chicken/veggie broth	10-12 oz. ribeye steak
1 lb. green beans	¼ cup pine nuts	1 pound salmon
1 leek	1 cup quinoa	6 oz. sausage (pick your meat)
4 lemons	1 small jar sundried tomatoes	
1 lime		8 oz. Smoked Sockeye Salmon
6 cups mixed greens	1 pack tortillas (or get lettuce)	1 lb. Talapia
5 small mushrooms	¼ cup walnuts (optional)	6 lb. whole chicken
2 onions		
1 orange		
1 bunch parsley		
4 plantains		
1 red onion		
1 shallot		
1 spaghetti squash		
2-3 cups spinach		
3 large sweet potatoes		

WEEK 2 SHOPPING LIST		
Produce	**Pantry**	**Meat**
1 lb. asparagus	8 cups almond flour	¼ lb. bacon
2-3 bananas	20 oz chicken broth	4-6 chicken thighs
2 large beets	2 cans coconut milk	1 lb. cube steak
1 head broccoli	1 small can diced serrano	27 eggs
1 large butternut squash	chiles (optional)	2 lb. ground beef
3 small head cauliflower	27 oz can diced tomatoes	6 oz. sausage
1 bunch fresh cilantro	½ - ¾ cup macadamia nuts	(pick your meat)
10 leaves fresh sage	1 small jar sundried	1 lb. trout
1 bag frozen mixed berries	tomatoes	1 lb. white fish
1 head garlic	¼ cup walnuts (optional)	
1 leek	½ gallon milk	
2 lemons	2 cups shredded cheese	
2 limes		
5 mini bell peppers		
4 cups mixed greens		
1 container mushrooms		
3 onions		
2 oranges		
1 bunch parsley		
4 pasilla peppers		
1 red bell pepper		
4-5 roma tomatoes		
2 cups spinach		
3 large sweet potatoes		
3-4 zucchini		

WEEK 3 SHOPPING LIST

Fruits and Veggies	Pantry	Meat
2-3 bananas	2 cups almond flour	2-4 slices bacon
1 bunch basil	1 small can bamboo shoots	3 lb. chicken hind
2 bunches bok choy	4 buns	quarters
1 lb. brussels sprouts	2 cans whole tomatoes	7 eggs
1 small head cauliflower	24 oz. chicken broth	3 lb. ground beef
2 ribs celery	¼ cup coconut flour	3 lb. pork tenderloin
1 cucumber	1 can coconut milk	1 lb. salmon
6 small eggplants	4 dried figs	1 lb. shrimp, small
few sprigs fresh dill	16 oz. pureed tomatoes	
1 bag frozen mixed berries	1 small jar red curry paste	
1 head garlic	¼ cup walnuts (optional)	
2 lemons	½ gallon milk	
2 cups mixed greens	2 cups shredded mozzarella	
5 onions		
2 bunches parsley		
1 bunch radishes		
3-4 roma tomatoes		
A few sprigs rosemary		
1 large sweet potato		
1 bunch swiss chard		
3-4 zucchinis		

SHOPPING LIST: STAPLES

- baking soda
- balsamic vinegar
- bbq sauce
- butter/coconut oil
- cashew butter
- ceyanne pepper
- cinnamon
- coriander
- cumin
- dijon mustard
- dried oregano
- dried sage
- garlic powder
- hemp protein
- honey
- marjoram
- olive oil
- paprika
- pepper
- poultry seasoning
- sea salt
- tapioca flour
- white vinegar

RECIPES

RECIPES

APPETIZERS
Cherl's Deviled Eggs
Salmon Boats
Mango Salsa
Cauli-Hummus
Bacon Wrapped Pineapple and Dates

SOUPS, SALADS, DRESSINGS, AND SAUCES
Broccoli "Cheddar" Soup
Tomato Bisque
Roasted Butternut Squash Soup
Chicken Soup
Arugula Fruit Salad
Marinara Sauce
Balsamic Vinaigrette

BREAKFAST & BRUNCH
Almond Pancakes
Quiche
Sweet Potato Hash w/Baked Eggs
Frittata
Berry Smoothie
Cashew Butter Smoothie

ENTREES

POULTRY
  Roast Chicken
  Chicken and Dumplings
  Lemon Pepper Chicken Breasts

FISH & SEAFOOD
  Fish Tacos
  White Fish with Macadamia Nuts and Orange
  Salmon with Lemon
  Orange Trout
  Shrimp Curry

MEAT
  Pork Tenderloin
  Eggplant Parmesan
  Beef Moussaka
  Broiled Steak
  Meatballs
  Stuffed Pasilla Peppers
  Fig Bacon Burger
  Pork Short Ribs
  Spaghetti Squash and Marinara Sauce
  Chicken Fried Steak
  Zucchini Lasagna

VEGGIES & SIDE DISHES
Mashed Plantains
Mashed Cauliflower
Baked Broccoli with Lemon
Sautéed Spinach and Pine Nuts
Mashed Sweet Potatoes
Sautéed Brussels Sprouts
Mexican Rice Style Quinoa
Rosemary Zucchini
Roasted Radishes
Sautéed Swiss Chard
Green Beans and Shallots
Lemon Asparagus
Cauliflower Rice
Tomato Cucumber Salad

DESSERTS
Bananas Foster
Sautéed Apples
Strawberry Banana Ice Cream
Chocolate Banana Nut Ice Cream

DRINKS & JUICES
Sangria
Watermelon Cucumber Juice
Carrot Parsley Juice
Mimosa
Orange, Mango, Carrot Goodness

APPETIZERS

Appetizers are the perfect goodies! They are the party favors of your meal! They are great for your dinner party or when your tribe comes over. I like to have my appetizers match the food I will be serving for dinner. If I am having pasta dinner with some meat, then the appetizers will be hummus with veggies and Greek olives, things of that nature. They are essentially the sprinkles of the perfect banana split, come in small bites and are appealing to the eyes. It also keeps the guests busy while you make the final touches on dinner. Bacon wraps are the greatest appetizers. Dips also make great appetizers and can be perfect for Super Bowl Parties and Taco Tuesdays.

Recipes included:

- Deviled Eggs
- Salmon Boats
- Mango Salsa
- Cauli-Hummus
- Bacon Wrapped Pineapple and Dates

Cherl's Deviled Eggs

Ingredients:

1 dozen eggs

2 tablespoons of white or apple cider vinegar

½ cup mayo

1 ½ tablespoons mustard

Salt and pepper to taste

Paprika

Tools:

Medium pot

Cutting board

Knife

Medium bowl

Fork

Measuring cups and spoons

Plate to serve

Directions:

1. Gently place eggs in medium pot.

2. Cover with water and add vinegar.

3. Place on stovetop and boil for 15 minutes.

4. When your timer dings, remove from stove and run your pot of eggs under cold water.

5. Peel your eggs.

6. Hot dog cut the eggs and place yolk in bowl.

7. Combine mayo, mustard, and salt and pepper and mash with a fork until creamy.

8. Spoon mixture into egg whites.

9. Sprinkle with paprika.

Options/Notes:

- Should you not want to use mayo, try substituting ½ a large avocado instead.

- Use any delicious mustard you like! Cherl recommends using a squirt of both yellow and brown mustards. Taste it to see if you like it.

- Have a thing for bacon? Cook some up and sprinkle it on top. Yum-o!

Serves: a party! Or 24 bits of heaven

Salmon Boats

Ingredients:

1 endive (they look like mini romaine lettuce but more tightly packed)
8 ounces smoked sockeye salmon
¼ red onion
Enough olive oil to drizzle
Pepper to taste
1 tablespoon capers (optional)

Tools:
Cutting board
Knife

Directions:

1. Chop the end of the endive that holds all of the leaves together.

2. Separate the leaves out and rinse.

3. Open the deliciously smoked salmon, and maybe steal a piece to make sure it is safe for consumption. This may be the most important thing you do all day.

4. Place a piece of salmon in each endive leaf.

5. Thinly slice your red onion and put a little bit in each boat.

6. If you like capers, sprinkle them on.

7. Drizzle your boats in olive oil.

8. Add pepper to the top if you like.

Serves: 2 adults

Mango Salsa

Ingredients:

1 ripe mango or 1 cup frozen mango, thawed

¼ cup red onion

1 tablespoon cilantro

2 tablespoons lime juice

2 tablespoons rice vinegar

1 jalapeno (optional)

Tools:

Cutting board

Knife

Small to medium bowl

Measuring spoon

Paring knife (optional, if using jalapeño)

Food processor (optional)

Mango corer and slicer (optional)

Directions:

1. Set the mango on the cutting board stem end down and hold. Place your knife about ¼ from the widest center line and cut down through the mango. Flip the mango around and repeat this cut on the other side. The resulting ovals of mango flesh are known as the "cheeks" and the mango seed left in the middle.

2. Cut parallel slices into the mango flesh, being careful not to cut through the skin. Turn the mango cheek a quarter rotation and cut another set of parallel slices to make a checkerboard pattern.

3. Here's where you can choose your favorite method. Either: "Slice and Scoop"— scoop the mango slices out of the mango skin using a large spoon—or "Inside Out"— turn the scored mango cheek inside out by pushing the skin up from underneath, and scrape the mango chunks off of the skin with a knife or spoon. Place in bowl.

4. Dice your red onion and cut up your cilantro. Add to bowl.

5. To juice your lime, cut it in half, open it, and stab the inside of the lime with a fork. Slightly twist the fork as you squeeze the outside. This gives you more juice.

6. Add the rice vinegar, and stir it all together.

7. If you like a finer salsa, you can pulse this in your food processor.

Options/Notes:

- If you want a sweeter salsa, use a sweet yellow onion.

- For a spicier salsa, add the jalapeño. If you wear contacts, please, please, for the love of all things holy, wear gloves, especially if you take them out at night! I made the mistake of not doing that only once and had burning eyeballs when I went to bed and then again the next morning when I put them in.. Now how to cut the jalapeño: cut the hat off first (that's the stem of it). Then make a hot dog cut all the way through. Open the spicy devil. With a small paring knife, cut out the seeds and membrane (the light green stuff).

- Do you eat mango all the time? If you do, then I highly recommend getting a mango corer to make your life a million times easier.

- Other great fruit options are peaches and pineapple. Mr. Shook recently got to sample a peach version and had his socks knocked off.

- **Serves:** 2 adults

*AUTHOR'S NOTE: I stole the directions for how to cut a mango from http://www.mango.org/how-cut-mango

Cauli-Hummus

Ingredients:

1 head of cauliflower, cut into florets
    (fancy way to say chop it up into 2" pieces)
1-2 lemons (this is up to your taste buds)
1-4 tablespoons tahini (a sesame paste)
½-2 cups olive oil
1-3 tablespoons cumin
Salt and pepper to taste
Enough water to cover bottom of pot

Tools:

Cutting board
Knife
Medium pot with lid
Food processor
Measuring cup and spoons
Steamer basket (optional)

Directions:

1. Fill your medium pot with about an inch of water and place your steamer basket inside. If you don't have one, see options/notes. Place lid on pot and put on high heat.

2. Cut cauliflower into florets. Remove the green stem first. Keep the pieces to about the size of your thumb so they cook evenly.

3. Your water should be boiling by now. Remove lid and place cauliflower in steamer basket. Replace lid.

4. Reduce heat to medium high.

5. Cook for 8-12 minutes. You'll know it is done when it gets a translucent looking and you can easily stab a fork through it.

6. Transfer cauliflower to food processor and add the rest of the ingredients, smaller quantities first. Blend on high until smooth. If the bigger pieces aren't blending, add more olive oil ¼ cup at a time until it starts to blend easily.

7. Take a taste and see if it needs anything. If it does, add it and then re-blend.

8. To serve, put in a cute dish, make a little volcano with the dip (think mashed potato volcano), and drizzle with olive oil. If you're feeling super fancy, sprinkle cumin on top. Serve with pita, cucumber slices, carrot sticks, or anything else that you would like and enjoy! I personally prefer crunch veggies with it.

Options/Notes:

- This recipe is all about your taste buds, which is why there is such a wide range of measurements. Start with the lower amount and then add more from there. Remember, have fun! This is all about YOU!

- If you don't have a steamer basket, no problem! Just fill your pot until the bottom inch is covered with water and voila! Instant steam.

- This is just a delicious base recipe. If you like garlic, you can always add roasted garlic and blend. You could do roasted red peppers, sun-dried tomatoes, or jalapeños and cilantro (wear gloves for the jalapenos!). Just add what you like!

Serves: 2 cups (or just enough to have a party)!

Bacon Wrapped Pineapple and Dates

Ingredients:

8 ounces dates
8 ounces pineapple, diced
1 pound sliced bacon, sliced in ½ or ⅓ depending on the length

Tools:

Cutting board
Knife
Tooth picks
Baking sheet
Tin foil

Directions:

1. Preheat oven to 350 degrees.

2. Line baking sheet with tin foil (only for ease of cleaning).

3. Slice dates in half and remove pit.

4. Chop pineapple into bite size pieces.

5. Wrap each piece of fruit in a bacon blanket and secure with a toothpick.

6. Bake for 20-25 minutes.

7. For the love of all things holy, please give these at least a couple minutes to cool off before you stick them in your mouth. The sugar in the fruit makes them nuclear hot when they come out of the oven.

Options/Notes:

- The measurements are just approximations. Also, the size of the pieces are up to you. I recommend doing bite size pieces that way no one has scalding fruit and bacon hitting their lower lip, and you don't have to deal with them getting angry with you. I may have learned that one the hard way.

Serves: a party of two very appetizer frenzied adults (protein and fruit makes for a whole meal-ish) OR a party

SOUPS, SALADS, DRESSINGS, AND SAUCES

Vegetable based soups are great for cold, winter days, while salads are fantastic on summer days with their refreshing crunch. Be brave and try your salads without drowning them in ranch and giving the balsamic vinaigrette a try!

Recipes included:

- Broccoli "Cheddar" Soup
- Tomato Bisque
- Roasted Butternut Squash Soup
- Chicken Soup
- Arugula Fruit Salad
- Beet Salad
- Marinara Sauce
- Balsamic Vinaigrette

Broccoli "Cheddar" Soup

Ingredients:

2 pounds broccoli, chopped

2 cups chicken broth

¼-1 cup nutritional yeast

½-1 cup canned coconut milk

Salt and pepper to taste

Tools:

Large pot with lid

Steamer basket

Cutting board

Knife

Food processor

Measuring cup

Directions:

1. In a large pot, place steamer basket at the bottom and fill until you can just see water at the bottom of the basket.

2. Place on stove top, cover with lid, and turn the heat on high.

3. When it starts to steam/boil, add chopped broccoli and reduce to medium high.

4. Cook for 8 minutes. To test if it is done, poke broccoli with a fork. If it pierces it, it's done. If not, cook for 2 more minutes and check again. Repeat until done.

5. Place broccoli in food processor and add some of your chicken broth. Blend until smooth, adding chicken broth until it is fully processed.

6. Starting with ¼ cup, add nutritional yeast and a dash of salt and pepper and blend until incorporated. Taste, and if you need more cheese flavor, add more yeast. Blend until you have a flavor you enjoy.

7. Remove steamer basket from pot and dump out water.

8. Return broccoli mix to the pot and add remaining chicken broth and coconut milk. Taste to see if you need more "cheese," salt, or pepper.

9. Heat on medium until it starts to bubble.

10. Ladle into a bowl and enjoy.

Options/Notes:

- Nutritional yeast is an awesome alternative to cheese if you have trouble with lactose. It provides a cheese flavor with none of the cramping and unpleasantness of cheese for some.

- If you want to add a little creaminess to this, just add a couple of tablespoons of butter at the end.

- If you love bacon, cook up a couple pieces and then crumble it on top.

Serves: 2 adults plus leftovers

Tomato Bisque

Ingredients:

2 tablespoons coconut oil

2 small red onions

8 cloves of garlic or 2 teaspoon of pre-chopped garlic

4 x 28 oz. cans whole tomatoes

14 basil leaves

Pinch of baking soda

2 cups chicken broth

1 can coconut milk

3 tablespoons of butter

Tools:

Knife

Cutting board

Large pot

Food processor or blender

Can opener

Directions:

1. Heat coconut oil in a large pot over medium heat.

2. Dice onion into thumbnail size pieces.

3. To see if oil is hot, wet the tip of a finger with water and let the water droplet fall into the pot. If it splatters, it is hot. Once hot, throw in onion and sauté until translucent.

4. Toss in garlic and sauté for a minute or two longer. Do not let the garlic brown because it will taste bitter.

5. Remove onion and garlic from pot and place in food processor. Add one can of tomatoes and blend until smooth.

6. Return to pot.

7. Add second can of tomatoes to food processor and blend until smooth. Add to pot gently (it splatters magnificently), and repeat for the remaining cans.

8. Add basil, pinch of baking soda, chicken broth, and coconut milk to pot. Cover and simmer for at least 30 minutes.

9. Before you serve, add 3 tablespoons of butter and let it melt.

10. To serve, ladle into bowls and garnish with basil if you have extra leaves.

Options/Notes:

- Love soup? Double or even triple the recipe and freeze the leftovers in mason jars.

- Don't do meat? Just use veggie broth instead.

Serves: 2 with leftovers

Roasted Butternut Squash Soup

Ingredients:

Soup:
1 large butternut squash, or 2 small
1-2 tablespoons coconut oil or butter (separate from below)
2 cups chicken broth
1 cup canned coconut milk
Salt and pepper to taste

Crispy sage:
4 tablespoons butter
10 sage leaves

Tools:

Vegetable peeler
Knife
Cutting board
Large spoon
Medium mixing bowl
Measuring cups and spoons
Food processor or blender
Large pot
Small frying pan

Directions:

1. Preheat oven to 400 degrees.

2. Peel the squash until you see dark orange.

3. Cut the ends of the squash.

4. Cut the squash long ways (hot dog) and open.

5. Scrap out the seeds using a large spoon.

6. Dice butternut squash into ¾" to 1" cubes.

7. Place diced squash into mixing bowl and coat with melted coconut oil/butter and salt and pepper.

8. Bake for a half hour.

9. At the end of that half hour, stab squash with a fork. If it is soft and goes into the cube, it's done. If not, continue to cook for 5 minutes and try again.

10. Once done, scoop cubes into your food processor and add a cup of chicken broth. Blend until smooth, adding more chicken broth to process if needed.

11. Pour blended squash into a large pot and add remaining chicken broth and coconut milk. Turn heat to medium low and cook for 15 minutes.

12. While the soup is stewing, wash your sage leaves and pat them dry.

13. In a small frying pan, melt 4 tablespoons of butter in one spot (this means don't swish it around). Heat at medium high.

14. When the butter starts to brown at the edges, reduce heat to medium, swirl butter around, and add sage leaves.

15. Continue to cook for 1-2 minutes, until crispy.

16. To serve, ladle soup into bowl and top with browned butter.

Options/Notes:

- Don't do meat? Not a problem, just use veggie broth instead of chicken.

Serves: 4 people

Chicken Soup

Ingredients:

2 tablespoons cooking fat (butter or coconut oil)

1 yellow onion

1 carrot, diced

1 teaspoon thyme

½ teaspoon oregano

2 garlic cloves, minced (or ½ teaspoon jarred chopped garlic)

2 pounds boneless, skinless chicken thighs, chopped

1 teaspoon salt

½ teaspoon ground black pepper

1 large sweet potato or yam

1 bunch of swiss chard

1 bay leaf

4 cups chicken broth

6 cups of water

1 lemon, juiced

Tools:

Knife

Cutting board

Large pot with lid

Measuring cups and spoons

Directions:

1. Heat a large pot over medium-high heat. Add cooking fat.

2. When hot, add onion, carrot, thyme, and oregano, and sauté for about 10 minutes, or until it is translucent.

3. While the vegetables sauté, cut up your chicken.

4. Add garlic and sauté for a minute longer.

5. Add chicken, salt, and pepper to veggie mixture and cook for 10 more minutes.

6. Then add the potato, chard, and bay leaf. Then fill with chicken broth and water (reverse order has everything splashing everywhere).

7. Put the lid on, and reduce to medium low for 20 minutes.

8. At the end of 20 minutes, remove lid, add lemon juice, and stir.

Options/Notes:

- Play with this one! Don't have a sweet potato but a white one? Use it instead. Want to get rid of your kale? Toss it in! This is a great recipe to clear out the veggies that are about to go bad.

Serves: 4 people with leftovers for lunch

Arugula Fruit Salad

<u>Ingredients:</u>

Salad:
4-5 cups arugula leaves
½ cup fresh pineapple or mango
1 avocado, diced
¼ red onion, thinly sliced
¾ cup macadamia nuts, chopped

Dressing:
Juice of large lemon
2 tablespoons apple cider vinegar
¼ cup olive oil
1 tablespoon Dijon mustard
1 teaspoon honey
Pepper to taste
Dash of garlic powder

<u>Tools:</u>

Cutting board
Knife
1 large bowl
1 small bowl
Hand mixer or whisk
Measuring spoons and cups

Directions:

1. Place all salad ingredients in a bowl.

2. Put all dressing ingredients in a small bowl and blend.

3. Pour dressing over salad or put it in one of those cute pouring devices.

Serves: 2 people

Beet Salad

Ingredients:

2 large beets or 4 small beets
¼-½ onion, sliced thinly
1 tablespoon olive oil
1-4 tablespoons lemon juice
Salt and pepper to taste

Tools:

Cutting board
Knife
Mixing bowl
Measuring spoon
Mixing spoon
Potato brush (optional)
Vegetable peeler (optional)

Directions:

1. Trim the top of the beet and the root. If you're picky, peel the beet. If not, use a potato brush to wash off the dirt.

2. Slice the beets and onion thinly and toss in bowl.

3. Add lemon juice, olive oil, and salt and pepper and toss.

4. Plate and nom!

Options/Notes:

• Start with the minimum of lemon juice and add more if you like.

Serves: 2 people

Marinara Sauce

Ingredients:

2-4 tablespoons olive oil

1 small red onion

4 cloves of garlic or 1 teaspoon of pre-chopped garlic

2 x 28 oz. cans whole tomatoes

Dried basil, to taste

Dried oregano, to taste

Pinch of baking soda

4-6 fresh basil leaves

4 tablespoons olive oil (for end)

1 pound ground meat (optional)

1 batch of homemade meatballs (optional)

1 pound Italian sausage (optional)

Tools:

Large pot

Cutting board

Knife

Food processor or blender

Directions:

1. Heat olive oil in a large pot over medium heat.

2. Dice onion into thumbnail size pieces.

3. To see if oil is hot, wet the tip of a finger with water and let droplet fall into the pot. If it splatters, it is hot. Once hot, throw in onion and sauté until translucent.

4. Toss in garlic and sauté for a minute or two longer. Do not let the garlic brown because it will taste bitter.

5. Remove onion and garlic from pot and place in food processor. Add one can of tomatoes and blend until smooth.

6. Return to pot.

7. Add second can of tomatoes to food processor and blend until smooth. Add to pot gently (it splatters magnificently).

8. Add basil, oregano, and pinch of baking soda (just a pinch!). Cover and simmer for at least 30 minutes.

9. If you like meat, add the cooked meat and let it simmer for about 30 minutes to incorporate flavors.

10. Right after you remove the sauce from heat and are about to serve it, drizzle the remaining 4 tablespoons of olive oil on top and chopped basil leaves. Stir to incorporate.

11. Serve with your favorite pasta-like things.

Options/Notes:

- Don't want to do wheat pasta? Not a problem! There are great bean pastas out there. You can also roast spaghetti squash or make "zoodles" (zucchini noodles) to use as spaghetti.

- This is another one where you can double or triple the recipe and freeze for later for spaghetti, pizza, or a rough base for tomato bisque. .

Serves: 4 people

Balsamic Vinaigrette

Ingredients:

¼ balsamic vinegar
½ teaspoon garlic powder
1 teaspoon thyme
1 teaspoon Dijon mustard
Salt and pepper to taste
1 cup olive oil
1 tablespoon lemon juice (optional)

Tools:

Hand blender or whisk
Tall measuring cup
Measuring spoon

Directions:

1. Put all ingredients except olive oil in measuring cup and blend/whisk.

2. Slowly drizzle olive oil in as you blend (this keeps it from separating when you store it)

3. Keeps for 3-5 days in the refrigerator.

Options/Notes:

- Try playing around with different vinegars to see what you like best.

Makes: 1 ¼ cups

BREAKFAST & BRUNCH

Breakfast:

Break down the term "breakfast" and you get break-fast. This means your body is fasting all night which can be eight to ten hours since we don't eat right before bed. When you don't grab breakfast, your body goes into the fight or flight phase which means it has to fight to survive and starts to store fats. This is caused by the body thinking you're starving the body. Waking up and drinking coffee also kicks the body into fight or flight mode. This is why you shouldn't drink coffee on an empty stomach, as there is nothing to absorb the acid from the coffee. Try fruits or protein shakes in the mornings instead. The best time to eat fruits is morning and afternoons. At night you don't want to eat fruits because your body will be digesting sugar while it sleeps instead of working through the protein and fat. Cereal and milk isn't the best breakfast, so substitute this with healthier choices, such as having a protein shake or preparing something the night before. Preparation is key in the entire process. Be kind to your system and don't freak out. You got this!

Brunch:

Brunch is all about feeling fancy and enjoying it since it's usually done on the weekend (I totally approve of you brunching any day of the week, truth be told). Think of dishes that are easy to throw together yet taste "sophisticated," stuff like smoked salmon and champagne. Champagne always comes out at my group's Tribal Brunch gatherings!

Recipes included:

- Almond Pancakes
- Quiche
- Sweet Potato Hash with Baked Eggs
- Frittata
- Berry Smoothie
- Cashew Butter Smoothie

Almond Pancakes

Ingredients:

2 eggs

¼ cup water

1 tablespoon coconut nectar, honey, or syrup

1 cup almond flour

¼ teaspoon salt

Coconut oil or butter for cooking

Browned banana, mashed (optional)

Handful of crushed walnuts (optional)

Tools:

Mixing bowl

Hand mixer

Measuring cups and spoons

Medium pan or griddle

Spatula

Rubber spatula, like the one you lick (optional)

Directions:

1. Break your eggs into the mixing bowl, and mix until they are light and fluffy. They should be a lovely shade of yellow and have bubbles.

2. Add water and coconut nectar/sweetener. Mix until incorporated.

3. Add almond flour and salt until blended.

4. If you are using banana and walnut, fold them in here. That just means mix gently with a rubber spatula until it's all blended.

5. Heat a medium pan (or griddle) on medium-high heat and add coconut oil or butter to melt.

6. Add spoonful of batter to your hot pan and cooked until browned. This should be about 3-5 minutes.

7. Flip and cook for another 2-3 minutes.

8. Keep the pancakes warm in your oven until you are ready to eat them all. Chomp!

Options/Notes:

- For almond flour, you can use ground almond flour or almond meal. The flour is a finer grain, while the meal is grainier.

- If the oil starts to smoke or your pancakes are a little too done, turn down the heat to medium.

- *Ideas for toppings:*
  sliced bananas and honey
  fresh berries and syrup
  orange zest, powdered sugar, and coconut nectar

Serves: 2 adults

Quiche

Ingredients:

Crust:
3 cup almond flour
½ teaspoon salt
¼ teaspoon garlic powder
½ teaspoon dried sage
4 tablespoons cold butter or coconut oil
1 egg

Filling:
1 tablespoon bacon fat
6 ounces' sausage (beef, pork, chicken, veggie, etc.)
½ cup chopped mushrooms
1 small leek, sliced
¼ cup sun-dried tomatoes, chopped
2 handfuls of greens
5 eggs
½ cup coconut milk (the canned kind)
½ teaspoon baking soda
2 tablespoons fresh parsley, minced
1 teaspoon fresh thyme, minced
Salt & pepper to taste

Tools:

Food processor
Measuring cups and spoons
Cutting board
Knife
Anti-stick spray
9" pie pan
Medium pan
Spatula

Directions:

1. Preheat oven to 350 degrees.

2. Mix all CRUST ingredients in food processor until well blended. NOTE: Don't worry about cleaning your food processor just yet!

3. Spray pie pan with anti-stick spray (I use a coconut oil one).

4. Press crust evenly into a pie pan. Get all up in there with the crust!

5. Bake crust alone 10-15 minutes, or until slightly browned.

6. While the crust is cooking, chop your veggies.

7. Heat the bacon fat in a medium pan over medium heat. Add sausage without casing, mushrooms, and leek. Sauté until sausage is browned and veggies are tender.

8. While your sausage and veggies are cooking, put the eggs, coconut milk, baking soda, parsley, thyme, salt, and pepper into your food processor and blend. NOTE: Once emptied, you can clean the food processor.

9. Toss your tomatoes and greens into the veggie mixture in the pan. Cook until you see the greens start to wilt, which is when they turn a darker green.

10. By this time, your crust will be done. Pull it out of the oven and place it on an even surface.

11. Put your sausage and veggie mixture into crust and spread it out evenly.

12. Gently pour the eggs over top and watch it get into the nooks and crannies.

13. Bake for 30-35 minutes until top of eggs are browned and eggs set (that means they don't jiggle. Jiggly eggs = uncooked.)

Options:

- Use any kind of sausage you like whether it is beef, pork, chicken, turkey, or veggie. To make it easier to cook, squeeze it out of the casing, which is the outer layer. If it is splitting while you're trying to squeeze it, cut one side lengthwise and use your fingers to get the meat off the lining.

- For the handfuls of veggies, you can use your favorite or just grab a baggie of already cleaned baby spinach, chard, and kale. It's yum-o and easy!

- Don't have a leek, use ¼ cup onion.

- If you've made the frittata, use some of the leftover bacon grease. If you don't have any, use coconut oil or butter instead.

- You can add whatever veggies you like. You could even use the veggies from the frittata in it!

- Honestly, I don't usually use fresh herbs. Feel free to use dried herbs if that's easier. For one, I hate chopping up thyme.

Serves: 2 adults with leftovers for 3 days or 8 people

Sweet Potato Hash w/Baked Eggs

Ingredients:

1 large sweet potato or 2 small/medium
1 tablespoon butter or coconut oil
4 eggs
Salt and pepper to taste

Tools:

Veggie/potato brush
Food processor with shredding disk (just makes it easier)
Measuring spoons
Oven safe medium pan or 2 personal tart pans

Directions:

1. Turn broiler on to high heat.

2. Wash sweeties with a brush under warm water.

3. Set sweeties aside, get medium sized oven safe pan out and heat oil/butter over medium heat.

4. Cut sweeties lengthwise to fit in processor.

5. Attach shredding disk to your food processor and shred on high speed.

6. Now that oil/butter is melted, add sweeties to pan.

7. Cook for 5-8 minutes, until soft.

8. When fully cooked, flatten out sweeties on the bottom of the pan, if oven safe. If not, place in personal tart pan.

9. Then create little dips or wells. This is where you will crack the eggs into.

10. Place pan with sweeties and eggs into the oven, uncovered.

11. Cook for 5-10 minutes, depending on how done you like your eggs.

12. Season with salt and pepper.

Options:

- Make the sweeties as a side dish for dinner by adding an extra potato or two. Then you can have the dish in the morning.

- Leave out eggs if you don't like them.

- If you're wanting some cheese, add a little to the top of the eggs before you put them in the broiler. Dairy or sans dairy is fine.

Serves: 2 adults

Frittata

Ingredients:

4 slices of thick bacon
½ onion
½-1 cup broccoli
1 small tomato or ½ large tomato
12 eggs
Salt and pepper to taste

Tools:

Medium pan
Spatula
Paper towel
Cutting board
Knife
Measuring cup
Mixing bowl
Whisk or fork
9" by 13" pan

Directions:

1. Preheat oven to 375 degrees.

2. In a medium pan over medium heat, cook bacon until it reaches the crispiness you enjoy.

3. While the bacon cooks, dice onion and chop broccoli to bite size pieces.

4. Remove bacon from pan and place on paper towel to de-grease.

5. Pour most of the bacon grease into a jar. Leave 1 table-spoon in the pan and add onion and broccoli. Cook until onion is translucent, 5-7 minutes.

6. While onions and broccoli are sautéing, chop tomato, crack eggs into a bowl and scramble, and chop bacon with either a knife or by hand. Salt and pepper eggs to taste.

7. Add tomato to scrambled eggs.

8. Now that onions and broccoli are cooked, add bacon to the pan and stir until combined.

9. Put onion, broccoli, bacon mixture into 9" by 13" pan.

10. Gently pour eggs over mixture.

11. Bake for 35-45 minutes, until cooked through. Cut the center to be sure it is done.

Options:

- Leave out the bacon (though according to my brother, who would do that?!) and use your favorite sausage.

- Add your favorite veggies. You can add anything you want!

- For Tribal Brunch, get pretty cupcake cups and bake in the cups. They'll be cute, decorative, and taste delicious!

Serves: 2 adults with leftovers for 2 days or six people

Berry Smoothie

Ingredients:

2¼ cups milk

1½ cups frozen berries

1 banana

6 tablespoons hemp protein powder

2 tablespoons diatomaceous earth (optional)

1 tablespoon bee pollen (optional)

Tools:

Blender

Directions:

1. Get out blender.

2. Put powders and pollen, if using, in there first.

3. Fill with berries, banana, and milk. The order is important! If you do liquid first, the solids will cause it to splatter.

4. Blend until smooth.

Options:

- Milk – use almond, coconut, cow, goat, human, whatever doesn't hurt your system.

- Frozen berries are a cost effective way to eat a whole bunch of berries any time of year. You can also use fresh berries if they're in season. With all berries, I recommend you eat organic, fresh or frozen, because they absorb pesticides so well.

Serves: 2 adults

Cashew Butter Smoothie

Ingredients:

2¼ cup milk

¼ cup cashew butter

1 banana

6 tablespoons hemp protein powder

2 tablespoons diatomaceous earth (optional)

1 tablespoon bee pollen (optional)

Tools:

Blender

Directions:

1. Get out blender.

2. Put powders and pollen, if using it, in there first.

3. Then fill with cashew, banana, and milk. The order is important! If you do liquid first, the solids will cause it to splatter.

4. Blend until smooth.

.

Options:

- Milk – use almond, coconut, cow, goat, human, whatever doesn't hurt your system.

- Cashew butter – substitute almond, macadamia nut, or sun butter. I choose to stay away from peanuts because they are generally heavily sprayed with pesticides.

Serves: 2 adults

ENTREES

POULTRY

Recipes included:

- Roast Chicken
- Chicken and Dumplings
- Lemon Pepper Chicken Breasts
- Ross' Mother Cluckin' BBQ Chicken
- Ross' Mother Cluckin' BBQ Chicken Caulizza

Roast Chicken

Ingredients:

1 onion
1-2 sweet potatoes
2 carrots
1 tablespoon thyme
1 tablespoon cooking fat
1 whole chicken, about 6 pounds
2-4 tablespoons butter
4 cloves garlic
1 lemon, sliced in half
Salt and pepper to taste
Cayenne pepper, just a sprinkle (optional)

Tools:

Vegetable peeler (optional)
Cutting board
Knife
Measuring spoon
Dutch oven or pan big enough for chicken
Tin foil (if not using Dutch oven)

Directions:

1. Preheat oven to 425 degrees.

2. Cut all of your vegetables into bite sized pieces.

3. Toss vegetables in bowl with cooking fat, salt, pepper, and a teaspoon of the thyme.

4. Place veggies in Dutch oven and set aside.

5. Remove the packaging off the bird. Stick your hands into the cavity to see if there are extra bits (well, they weren't extra when the chicken was alive, but you know…). These "extras" can be set aside for making chicken broth, compost, or you can toss them.

6. Rinse out the bird, inside and outside. Then dry it off with paper towels.

7. Very gently, slip your fingers underneath the chicken skin to loosen it up. Take pieces of butter and distribute it throughout the chicken, under the skin. This is part of what makes the meat so deliciously juicy.

8. Stuff the inside of the chicken with the lemon and garlic.

9. Top the vegetables with the chicken, booby side up.

10. Sprinkle with remaining thyme, salt, pepper, and should you choose to go with a little extra, a bit of cayenne.

11. Bake for about 1 hour and 20 minutes or until it is 165 degrees. Take the temperature from the thigh and avoid touching the bone (they get hotter than the meat).

12. Let it sit for 15 minutes (this keeps the juice inside the meat, just like with steak).

Options/Notes:

- You can use any root vegetables or squash you want. In the fall, I use butternut squash in there. Lighter vegetables, like greens, will not do. You want something that is roughly the texture of potatoes.

Serves: 4 adults with some leftovers

Chicken and Dumplings

<u>Ingredients:</u>

Soup:
1 small onion, peeled and diced
2 ribs of celery, diced
3 pounds of chicken with skin and bones (see notes)
1 ½ teaspoon of poultry seasoning
2 tablespoons of curly parsley, diced
1 teaspoon salt
3 cups of water
3 cups chicken broth
2 tablespoons of tapioca flour or arrowroot
½ cup of milk of choice (see notes)

Dumplings:
1 ½ cups of blanched, slivered almonds OR 1 ¼ almond flour (see notes)
½ teaspoon of salt
⅓ cup of broth from soup

<u>Tools:</u>

Cutting board
Knife
Medium to large pot with lid
Measuring cup and spoons
Slotted spoon

Medium bowl

2 forks

Small bowl or coffee mug

Food processor

Directions:

1. Chop your veggies to bite size pieces.

2. Heat a medium to large size pot on medium heat, add chicken, onions, celery, poultry seasoning, parsley, and salt. Cover with water and chicken broth (doing in reverse order leads to lots of splashing around). Cover and cook for 45 minutes.

3. Reduce heat to low.

4. Using a slotted spoon, gently remove chicken from pot and place in a bowl or on a cutting board. At this point it should be falling apart (yum)!

5. Use two forks to remove the meat from the bones and shred to bite size pieces.

6. In a small bowl or mug, mix the milk and flour to make what is called a slurry (now we're getting technical)! You can even use one of your chicken forks to cut down on clean up.

7. Add slurry to soup and stir thoroughly. This thickens the soup.

8. While that settles and thickens, add the almonds to your food processor and grind until they form a fine flour (only if you're using almonds). Skip this step is you are using ready-made flour.

9. Add salt and pulse for 30 seconds.

10. Using a measuring cup, steal the ⅓ cup of broth from your soup pot (it's not really stealing since you're going to give it back).

11. Blend until you have a beautiful, soft dough.

12. Using your hands, roll the dough into little balls. I like half-size balls that way I do not have to cut them and can just pop them in my mouth. That and I feel like I get more.

13. As you make the balls, drop them into the soup gently, stir in, and cook for an additional 15 minutes with the lid on.

Options/Notes:

- For the chicken, I prefer to use dark meat for the juiciness. If you prefer breast meat, that's fine, too.

- For the milk option, I prefer to use canned coconut milk so that it is creamier. I'm also unable to tolerate real dairy, so this is a great option for me.

- Tapioca flour is usually easy to find in the baking aisle of most grocery stores. If you can't find it and are interested in using it, you can always order it from Amazon.

- What's the difference between almond meal and almond flour? The meal tends to be a bit courser while the flour has a finer texture. I prefer to use the flour, specifically Bob's Red Mill brand.

- When it comes to bowls and pots, always go bigger. It is better to have the extra room and clean only one bowl/pot rather than starting too small, having to stop what you're doing, and scale up. Then you have to clean both!

- A food processor is the preferred tool here for the dough. The shape allows for more movement for the dough, which I like. With a blender, I have to constantly stop it and move stuff around.

Serves: 4 adults and leftovers

Lemon Pepper Chicken Breasts

Ingredients:

Marinade:
¼ cup lemon juice
1 tablespoon coarsely ground pepper
Salt to taste
½ cup olive oil

Gremolata:
3-4 garlic cloves
1 teaspoon lemon zest
1 tablespoon fresh parsley
3-4 whole chicken breasts, boneless skinless

Tools:

Whisk
Measuring cups
Meat mallet
Cutting board
Plastic bag or container with lid
Baking sheet
Tin foil (for ease of cleaning)
Knife
Food processor
Spoon – for the fancy stuff
Wine / wineglass (optional)

Directions:

1. Whisk together lemon juice, pepper, and salt.

2. In a slow stream, add olive oil to mixture to emulsify it (that simply means to blend oil and water until they are well combined).

3. Use a meat mallet, beat chicken until it is ¼" thick. I find that it helps to yell "Hi-ya!" as I'm doing this.

4. Place chicken boobs in a bag or containter with lid and add marinade. Seal bag before you even think about picking it up. Let marinade for 30 minutes. This is the perfect time to have a glass of wine while you wait, perhaps a Sauvignon Blanc.

5. After your 30 minutes are up and your wine is gone, turn oven broiler on high.

6. Place chicken on baking sheet and broil for 5-10 minutes on each side, depending on how dead you beat it. Not so dead gets longer. Super dead dead is shorter cooking time.

7. As the chicken is cooking, place your gremolata ingredients in a food processor and blend until you like the texture. To be honest, I do a little extra of everything that way there's no way I'm running out of the goodness.

8. To serve, just put the fancy stuff on top of the boobies.

Options/Notes:

- According to Merriam-Webster, gremolata is a seasoning mixture usually consisting of grated lemon zest, minced garlic, and minced parsley that is used especially with osso buco.

- If it's hot, and you'd rather grill, that is also a cooking option. Or the zombie apocalypse and the only option is outdoor cooking. At least you will have fine dining in your hideaway camp.

Serves: 4 adults

Ross' Mother Cluckin' BBQ Chicken
by Ross D'Agostaro, Super Little Brother

Ingredients:

Chicken parts, yo! (however much you want to shove in your face hole. Whatever type of chicken part is up to you. I prefer thighs with the skin still on to hold the flavor in.)

Your absolute favorite BBQ sauce (Sweet Baby Rays is the shit, just sayin')

Garlic powder, Bitches! And lots of it!

Cayenne powder

Thyme (everyone could use a little extra thyme in their lives)

Pepper

Instructions:

1. First off, clean your chicken parts and make sure they're looking pretty. No one wants to eat an ugly bird. Preheat that oven to a toasty 400 degrees (that's roughly 205 degrees C for all you others outside the U.S.).

2. After the chicken parts are primped and pretty, go ahead and use however much seasoning you like on the bird. If you like it spicy, slap some extra cayenne on there. Like it garlicy? You know what to do.

3. Throw those bad boys on a pan and let them cook for about 30-45 minutes, depending on the size and weight of the chicken parts.

4. After the time is up, pull the bird out and try your hardest to drown the chicken and BBQ sauce. Seriously. You can't go wrong with that shit. Coat it on there, thick. You'll thank me later.

5. Once you got the parts nice and BBQ-y, go ahead and throw them back in the oven for another 15 minutes. This will make the skin have a nice crisp and blend all the flavors together with the BBQ sauce.

Depending on how much chicken you made, it will last you several meals. If you like it a fair amount, it goes amazingly well on my Caulizza. Recipe on the next page.

Ross' Mother Cluckin' BBQ Chicken Caulizza
by Ross D'Agostaro, Super Little Brother

Ingredients:

1 head of cauliflower

Half of a yellow onion

2 handfuls of spinach

3 cloves of garlic

3 eggs

1 cup of almond meal/flour

Half of a red pepper, sliced

2 Roma tomatoes, whatever cut you prefer

Some kick ass BBQ chicken that you made from the night before but shredded by hand, still cold

Your favorite BBQ sauce (again, Sweet Baby Rays or GTFO)

1 big fucking bowl

Instructions:

1. Turn on the oven and crank it up to sweltering 350 degrees

2. Go ahead and get your food processor out chop up the cauliflower, onion, spinach, and garlic. Really chop them up (don't do it all at the same time. I did that and it was awful. Food was everywhere. Save yourself the trouble).

3. After everything has been chopped to absolute hell, throw it in a bowl and crack the 3 eggs on top of everything. Here's the fun part, reach in and mix everything by hand. While mixing, slowly pour the almond meal/flour into the mixture. Make sure clumps aren't created. No one wants clumpy pizza

4. Got everything mixed? Good. Throw it on a pan that has been prepped and form it into whatever caulizza crust shape you fancy (be creative!)

5. Once the "dough" is in your preferred shape, put it in the sweltering over for 15-20 minutes, depending on size, thickness, and shape. It should have a slight crisp look to the edges

6. After the time is up, pull it out of the over and add the red pepper, tomatoes, and most importantly, that awesome chicken that is shredded. Remember that I asked you to get extra BBQ sauce? Drizzle a good amount of that on there. Bitches love BBQ sauce. I love a lot of BBQ sauce, so I use a lot of it (I just referred to myself as a bitch...dammit).

7. Throw that epic caulizza back in the oven for about 15 minutes. Once you pull it out, that bitch should be ready to go into your face hole.

FISH & SEAFOOD

Recipes included:

- Fish Tacos
- White Fish w/ Macadamia Nuts and Orange
- Salmon w/ Lemon
- Orange Trout
- Shrimp Curry

Fish Tacos

Ingredients:

1-pound tilapia
1 lime, juiced
1 orange, juiced
1-2 tablespoons cumin
Salt, to taste
1 tablespoon coconut oil
Tortillas, gluten, gluten free or lettuce

Tools:

Cutting board
Knife
Plastic baggie or container with lid
Large pan
Spatula

Directions:

1. Put tilapia, lime juice, orange juice, cumin, and salt in a bag or a container with lid. Marinate for at least a half hour.

2. In a large pan, heat coconut oil over medium heat.

3. Add tilapia and half the juice.

4. As the fish cooks, start breaking it up into bite size pieces. This whole process will take about 5 minutes.

5. When the fish is done, put in the tortilla of your choice and serve with other yumminess, such as Mexican Quinoa and Mango Salsa.

Options/Notes:

- There are several different options when it comes to tortillas, gluten or sans gluten. Use whatever makes you happy. I recommend lettuce tacos.

- Funny story: my brother and I call these "Oh Man Tacos." The first time I made them with the Mexican Quinoa, I put them in my pie hole and sat there for probably the next five minutes just saying, "Oh man oh man oh man." When Ross, my brother, comes to visit me, he asks for them by name, Oh Man Tacos.

Serves: 2 adults

White Fish with Macadamia Nuts and Orange

Ingredients:

1 -pound white fish, such as sole
½-¾ cup macadamia nuts
1 orange, zested
1 tablespoon coconut oil or butter
Salt and pepper, to taste

Tools:

Baking sheet
Tin foil (ease of cleaning)
Lemon zester
Food processor
Measuring spoon

Directions:

1. Turn broiler on high.

2. Place tin foil on baking sheet and place fish on it.

3. Sprinkle fish with salt and pepper.

4. In a food processor, blend macadamia nut and orange zest until it is the texture of coarse sand.

5. Top the fish with the nut and orange mixture.

6. Add the cooking oil to the pan. Put a little between each piece of fish.

7. Broil for 6-10 minutes, depending on how thick the fish is. For this dish, you don't want the fish super close to the broiler as it will burn the nuts. Instead of the top rack, try having it set one below that.

Options/Notes:

• I'm a big fan of talking to people (surprise!), so I'll often ask the person at the meat counter what a good white fish of the day is. This dish is great with a flakey white fish. Play around and see what you like.

Serves: 2 adults

Salmon with Lemon

Ingredients:

1-pound fresh salmon
Fresh dill (dried also works)
Salt and pepper to taste
1 lemon
1 tablespoon cooking fat (butter or coconut oil work best)

Tools:

Baking sheet
Tin foil (ease of cleaning)
Cutting board
Knife
Measuring spoon

Directions:

1. Turn broiler on high.

2. Place tin foil on baking sheet and place fish on it, skin side down if you got one with skin.

3. Sprinkle fish with dill, salt, and pepper.

4. Thinly slice lemon and place over salmon. I like to make patterns with the lemon slices.

5. Add the cooking oil to the pan.

6. Broil for 10-15 minutes, depending on how thick the fish is. You'll know when it's done when it flakes apart.

Options/Notes:

- You can eat the skin of the fish if you like. I do, but it grosses my mom out, so of course I'm sure to eat it in front of her.

- If it is in your budget, get wild caught salmon. The farm fish can have antibiotics and other gross things in it. They also add some orange to it to make it look more like salmon "should" look. The wild salmon has a buttery taste to boot.

Serves: 2 adults

Orange Trout

Ingredients:

1-pound trout
Thyme (fresh if you've got it)
Salt and pepper to taste
1 orange
1 tablespoon butter or cooking oil

Tools:

Baking sheet
Tin foil (ease of cleaning)
Cutting board
Knife
Measuring spoon

Directions:

1. Turn the broiler on high.

2. If you dislike washing dishes as much as I do (and I really, really, really dislike it), cover a pan with tin foil and lay your fish on it, skin side down.

3. Sprinkle with salt, pepper, and thyme.

4. Slice your orange thinly and cover the fish with it, maybe make some patterns with the slices.

5. Add the cooking oil to the pan.

6. Broil for about 10 minutes or until it flakes.

7. Plate it, grab your favorite beverage (I enjoy it with a delicious pinot noir), and bon appétit!

Shrimp Curry

Ingredients:

1 small eggplant
1 small onion
1-2 tablespoons coconut oil
1-2 tablespoons red curry paste
1 small can bamboo shoots
2 bunches of bok choy
1-pound shrimp
1 can of coconut milk
¼ cup fresh basil, sliced
2 tablespoons fish sauce (optional)

Tools:

Cutting board
Knife
Large pan

Directions:

1. Slice all veggies into bite size pieces.

2. Heat large pan over medium heat and add coconut oil when hot.

3. Add eggplant and onion to pan. Sauté for 8 minutes

4. Add curry paste cook until well mixed.

5. Add remaining ingredients, bamboo shoots, bok choy, shrimp, coconut milk, basil, and fish sauce (if using).

6. Cook for 3-5 minutes until shrimp are pink and cooked.

7. Serve over rice or cauli-rice.

Options/Notes:

- Depending on how much time I have (see also: how much work I really want to do), I will buy the precooked, peeled shrimps. Not quite as good as fresh, but they totally work in a pinch.

Serves: 2 adults with leftovers

MEAT

Recipes included:

- Pork Tenderloin
- Eggplant Parmesan
- Beef Moussaka
- Broiled Steak
- Meatballs
- Stuffed Pasilla Peppers
- Fig Bacon Burger
- Pork Short Ribs
- Spaghetti Squash and Marinara Sauce
- Chicken Fried Steak
- Zucchini Lasagna

Pork Tenderloin

Ingredients:

2-3 tablespoons coconut oil

3 pounds pork tenderloin

½ teaspoon salt

Pepper, to taste

¼ teaspoon ground sage

¼ teaspoon dried thyme

1 onion

Tools:

Cast iron pan. (Can use pan for stovetop and a baking sheet.)

Measuring spoons

Tongs or spatula

Cutting board

Knife

Tin foil or lid

Directions:

1. Preheat oven to 425 degrees.

2. Heat oil in the cast iron pan on medium high. Be careful of splashing.

3. Rub the spices into the meat. Get all up in there.

4. When the oil is hot, **gently** place the pork in the pan. Brown each side for about 3 minutes on each side (this seals in the juices).

5. As the meat is searing, slice your onion thinly.

6. When you've seared all sides of the meat, turn off the burner and add the onion to the pan.

7. Cover with lid or tin foil and place in oven. Bake for 30-50 minutes, depending on the thickness of the meat. Start with 30 minutes first. If it is not done, check in another 5 minutes, so on and so forth. It should reach an internal temperature of 145 degrees.

8. Remove the pork from the oven and let rest covered for 5-10 minutes. Then cut.

Options/Notes:

- I like to use a cast iron pan because it can go directly from stovetop to oven. Another option is to use a Dutch oven. If neither of those are available to you, all you need is a pan to sear the meat and a baking pan.

- Letting the meat rest allows for the juice to stay in the meat fibers rather than running down your cutting board and making a mess.

Serves: 2 adults with leftovers

Eggplant Parmesan

Ingredients:

2 eggplants
Salt
¼-½ cup coconut oil
4-6 cups marinara sauce, preferably your own
Mozzarella cheese or non-dairy alternative
Pepper, to taste
1-pound ground meat or tofu(optional)

Tools:

Veggie pealer (optional)
Mandolin (if you have one, or use a knife and cutting board)
Colander
9"x13" pan
Measuring cup

Directions:

1. An hour before preparing, peel eggplant (optional really), and slice into ¼ to ½ rounds. Place eggplant in colander and sprinkle with salt. Let sit for 45 minutes to 1 hour.

2. Rinse eggplant and pat dry.

3. Preheat the oven to 375.

4. In the baking pan, put a layer of marinara sauce, eggplant, and then cheese. Repeat this until you have reached the top. If you are using meat, layer it on top of your eggplant layers (sauce, eggplant, protein, cheese, repeat.)

5. Bake for 30-45 minutes. Be careful when you start to shove it in your mouth because it will be nuclear hot.

Options/Notes:

• If you cannot handle dairy products, leave the dairy out. You can also use a lactose free or vegan alternative.

• If you'd like something a little different, you can use zucchini instead of, or in addition to, the eggplant.

Serves: 2 adults with leftovers

Beef Moussaka

<u>Ingredients:</u>

The base:
3 eggplants
Olive oil, to taste
3 onions, cut in half and then sliced
4 cloves of garlic, minced
2 pounds ground beef
1 bunch chopped parsley
1 tablespoon dried oregano
Salt and pepper, to taste
2 cups pureed tomatoes

Bechamel Sauce:
¼ cup coconut flour
1 tablespoon almond flour (don't use meal because it's too thick)
1 egg, beaten
½ teaspoon paprika
Freshly ground pepper

<u>Tools:</u>

Vegetable peeler
Mandolin (if you have one. If not, use a knife.)
Cutting board
Knife

Colander

Heavy item, such as a sack of flour or jar of almond butter

2 large pans

Spatula

Paper towel or CLEAN dishrag

Anti-stick spray

9"x13" pan

Directions:

1. About 45 minutes before you plan to start cooking, cut the ends off the eggplant and peel stripes along the skin. There should be an inch of skin for every half inch of peeled eggplant, just like candy cane stripes.

2. Slice the eggplant about 1/2" thick. I used 3/8" on my mandolin, which makes the job go by so much quicker, but use the guard! In all seriousness, I'm still missing the edge of my right thumb beause I was too cool for the guard.

3. Stack the eggplant Lincoln Log style in a colander. Salt each layer. What this does is draw out the natural liquids in the eggplant.

4. Turn a plate upside down on top of the eggplant, and secure with a heavy item.

5. After 40 minutes or so, preheat the oven to 400 degrees.

6. Heat up some olive oil in a pan at medium heat, and add onions. Yes, we usually use coconut oil because of the higher smoke point, but I prefer to use olive oil in my traditional dishes because it tastes like home to me.

7. Once the onions have become translucent, add garlic and sauté for a minute.

8. Add beef, a handful of parsley, oregano, salt, and pepper. I smell the mixture to see if I have added enough spice. There's no way for me to be more specific. Just feel it out and go with it. If it smells good to you, you've done it right. Sauté until most of the juice has evaporated out, about 15-20 minutes.

9. Add the pureed tomatoes and simmer on medium heat for 20 minutes. This will reduce the sauce, meaning it will be thicker and less watery.

10. Towards the end of the simmer, go back to your eggplant and rinse them all off. Pat them dry with paper towels or clean dishrag.

11. Fry up the eggplant in batches by adding a little oil to the pan and cooking for about 3 minutes on each side.

12. Spray your 9"x13" pan with anti-stick spray, and then layer it: eggplant, meat sauce, eggplant, meat sauce, eggplant, meat sauce.

13. Put the main part of the dish aside to work on the sauce. Add all the ingredients to a medium pot and put on medium high heat.

14. Mix continually, cook until the consistency of porridge or thick oatmeal.

15. Top the casserole with the freshly cooked sauce.

16. Bake for 30 minutes.

17. Let it cool slightly so you don't burn yourself, and then enjoy.

Serves: 2 adults with leftovers for a couple of days

Broiled Steak

Ingredients:

2 beef steaks, 5-6 oz. each (rib eyes are my favorite, but you
    can also use sirloin, strip, and tenderloin)
Dried oregano, to taste
Black pepper, to taste
Garlic powder, to taste
Salt, to taste
1-2 tablespoons coconut oil

Tools:

Baking pan
Tin foil
Tablespoon

Directions:

1. Take steaks out of fridge and let sit for a half hour to warm up a bit (this allows them to cook much nicer).

2. Preheat the broiler to high. Place one oven rack to the highest setting or the one just below that.

3. Line baking pan with tin foil (for ease of cleaning).

4. Place steaks on foil lined pan.

5. Sprinkle both sides of the steaks with your herbs.

6. Dollop coconut oil on top of them.

7. Broil steaks for 7 minutes for medium rare (8 minutes for medium).

8. Flip steaks to unbroiled side and cook the other side for an additional 5 minutes for medium rare (6 minutes for medium).

9. When it reaches your favorite doneness, remove from oven, cover in foil (or make a foil tent) and rest for 5 minutes.

10. Cut your steaks into whatever size pieces make you the happiest!

Options/Notes:

- The reason you let the meat rest is so that less juices are lost when you cut into it. This makes each piece that much juicier, that much more delicious.

- I like the rib-eye because it has more fat content and tastes delicious, especially with a grass fed cow, which picks up the flavors of the greens the cow eats. Do some research, play around, and see what kind of steak you like the best. There are many online companies that will deliver grass fed beef to your door. Most grocery stores are also now catering to people choosing to eat higher quality meats.

Serves: 2 adults

Meatballs

<u>Ingredients:</u>

2 pounds ground beef

1-2 teaspoon parsley

½-1 teaspoon basil

½-1 teaspoon oregano

¾ teaspoon salt

2 tablespoons cooking fat (I'm a purist and use olive oil, despite it not being as great for you when hot)

½-1 onion, diced

3 cloves of garlic

Paprika and red pepper flakes, to taste (optional)

<u>Tools:</u>

Bowl

Measuring spoons

Cutting board

Knife

Medium pan

Anti-stick spray

Baking sheet

Directions:

1. Preheat oven to 350 degrees.

2. Put your meat and spices in a bowl.

3. Dice your onion into small pieces. These will be going into the meatballs, so you choose how big you want the pieces going into your mouth with each bite. That being said, I like them diced finely.

4. Heat your pan to medium and add cooking fat.

5. When hot, add the onion and sauté until translucent.

6. While the onion cooks, dice your garlic, or use a teaspoon of the already minced kind. It's my fav!

7. Add garlic to pan and sauté for a minute or two. You'll want to stop before the garlic turns brown, which will make it taste funky and bitter.

8. Add onion and garlic to the meat mixture. Let cool for a moment.

9. While your meat mixture cools, spray the baking pan with an anti-stickum spray.

10. You'll be getting down and dirty, so remove your rings, wash your hands, and get your hands all up in the bowl to mix everything together.

11. Form meatballs 1-2" in diameter and place on pan. The smaller you make them, the quicker they cook and the less cutting you have to do on your plate.

12. Cook for 30 minutes in oven.

Options/Notes:

- Add these to your favorite sauce, freeze some for later, or make a sub sandwich with a little bit of marinara sauce. If you are serving marinara sauce with these, be sure to let the sauce incorporate the meat into it. I like to give the sauce at least an hour to have the meatballs in there.

Serves: 24 meatballs – how many can you chow down?

Stuffed Pasilla Peppers

Ingredients:

4 pasilla peppers
1-pound ground beef
Juice of two limes
1 tablespoon cooking fat
½ onion
5 mini bell peppers
½ teaspoon salt
2 tablespoons fresh cilantro, chopped
2 cloves garlic
1 tablespoon balsamic vinegar
½ teaspoon coriander
½ teaspoon cumin
½ teaspoon oregano
Diced serrano peppers (optional)
Couple of handfuls of cheese (optional)

Tools:

Baking sheet
Tin foil
Timer
Medium pan
Spatula
Bowl for beef
Bowl for peppers

Plastic wrap or clean towel

Cutting board

Knife

Measuring spoon

Directions:

1. Set your oven broiler on high and line a baking sheet with aluminum foil.

2. Place your pasilla peppers on the baking sheet and place under the broiler.

3. Turn the pasilla peppers every 5-7 minutes. Set a timer!

4. While the peppers cook, heat up your pan on medium.

5. Brown ground beef. When it is fully cooked, add half the lime juice and mix it in. Put in separate bowl.

6. By now, your peppers should be fully browned and have cracked skin. Put them in a bowl and cover with plastic wrap or a clean towel.

7. While the peppers sit, heat the cooking fat. Once hot, add onion and mini bell peppers. Cook until onions are translucent.

8. Add the beef, cilantro, garlic, balsamic vinegar, coriander, cumin, and oregano. If you are using serrano peppers, add them here. Cook for 2 minutes, get it all mixed.

9. Remove beef from heat.

10. Peel the skin off of the peppers using your hands. Remove the stem and seeds.

11. Stuff the peppers with your meat mixture.

12. If using the cheese, add a bit to each pepper. Then put it back under the broiler for a couple of minutes to get it delicious and melty. If you don't use the cheese, still put them under the broiler to warm the peppers back up.

Options/Notes:

- If you don't have coriander, you can double the cumin instead.

- For the cheese, you can use anything you want. My household cannot do dairy, so we use our favorite vegan cheese from Follow Your Heart.

- If you have meat leftovers, you can save them for the next day and have tacos!

- You can always double the meat portion to ensure you have leftovers to make tacos the next day.

Serves: 2 adults with leftovers

Fig Bacon Burger

Ingredients:

1-pound ground beef
2-4 slices bacon
4 dried figs
Salt and pepper, to taste

Tools:

Bowl
Cutting board
Knife
Medium pan
Slotted spoon
Paper towel
Oil jar
Spatula

Directions:

1. Get all of your ingredients out and place on the counter.

2. Open the beef and place in your bowl.

3. Chop up your raw bacon.

4. Heat up your pan to medium heat and add bacon. Cook until you like the level of doneness.

5. While the bacon cooks, chop the figs finely and add to ground beef.

6. When bacon is done, use a slotted spoon to take it out of the pan. Place it on a paper towel. Blot bacon to remove excess grease.

7. Add bacon to beef mixture and let cool for a minute or two.

8. While the bacon cools, VERY CAREFULLY pour the bacon grease into a jar. It should not go down your drain as it can cause clogs. It's actually really great to use the bacon grease for other dishes. Keep in mind, a little goes a long way!

9. Remove any rings you may be wearing, wash your hands, and get ready to get down and dirty! Mix everything together, adding salt and pepper if you'd like.

10. Split the meat into four even rounds. Manhandle it until you form little patties (there are tools to do this for you if you'd like, but I just use my hands). Leave a thumb indention on one side so that it cooks evenly.

11. Heat pan to medium high, a little of the bacon grease in there is fine, and place the burgers on when it is hot. To test, get a drop of water, and then drop it on the pan. If it sizzles, it's good to go.

12. Cook them 4-6 minutes on each side, depending on how done or not done you prefer your cow.

13. Serve with your favorite bun or lettuce wrap and add your favorite toppings. Please promise me you won't add ketchup.

Options/Notes:

- For buns, there are plenty of options. Boston lettuce and iceberg lettuce are great options. If you'd prefer the bun, there are several varieties full of gluten or not. The options are endless.

- Tired of beef? Try bison or buffalo instead! I'm not brave enough (yet), but there is a grocery store near me that sells ground kangaroo and ostrich. One of these days I will give them a try.

Serves: 2 adults with leftovers

Pork Short Ribs

WARNING: This recipe involves overnight work!!!

Ingredients:

3-4 pounds pork short ribs
2 cups white vinegar
2 cups water
Your favorite barbecue sauce

Tools:

Gallon sized plastic bag
Measuring cup
Bowl
Slow cooker
Fork

Directions:

1. The night before you plan to eat your ribs, put them in a plastic baggie and add water and vinegar.

2. Set it in a bowl, so you don't get juice everywhere in case you didn't fully seal it.

3. The next morning, drain the bag. Remove the ribs and rinse them off.

4. Put the ribs directly into the slow cooker.

5. Add your favorite barbecue sauce until they are covered. Then add a little bit extra, just to be sure.

6. Cook on low for 6-8 hours. We often eat these without the bones since they just fall right out.

Options/Notes:

- Why "vinegarize" your meat? This helps break down the meat fibers, thus making it more tender. YUM!

Serves: 2 adults with leftovers

Spaghetti Squash and Marinara Sauce

Ingredients:

1 spaghetti squash, medium to large
6 cups marinara sauce, preferably your own
1 pound of ground meat (optional)
1 batch of homemade meatballs (optional)

Tools:

Medium pan, if using meat
Cutting board
Knife
Spoon
Slow cooker
Fork

Directions:

1. If you are using meat, sauté it in a pan until fully cooked.

2. Cut the spaghetti hamburger style.

3. Spoon out the seeds.

4. Put your marinara sauce in your slow cooker. Add meat and stir.

5. Add your spaghetti squash, cut side down. When you look into the slow cooker, it should look like boobies sticking out of marinara sauce.

6. Cook on low for 4-6 hours.

7. To know when it is done, very carefully pull out the spaghetti squash. Gently use a fork on the inside flesh to scrape the "spaghetti." If it is hard, it needs more cooking time. If it starts flaking out and looks like spaghetti, you're done!

Options/Notes:

- You know the scrapers they sell at pumpkin patches to get rid of the pumpkin seeds? This is the perfect device to scrap out squash seeds year round! If you don't have one, just use a spoon.

Serves: 2 adults with leftovers

Chicken Fried Steak

Ingredients:

1 cup tapioca flour
1 teaspoon salt
1 teaspoon garlic powder
2 eggs, beaten
1 pound cube steak
¼ cup to 1 cup of coconut oil for frying
½ cup canned coconut milk
Dash of cayenne in powder mixture (optional)

Tools:

2 wide bowls
Measuring spoons and cups
2 forks
Large pan
Spatula
Cookie cooling rack (optional really)
Whisk

Directions:

1. Combine tapioca flour, salt, and garlic powder (and cayenne, if using) in a wide dish.

2. In a separate wide bowl, beat the eggs until well blended.

3. In a large pan, heat the coconut oil ¼ cup at a time.

4. Dredge the cube steak through the egg mixture and then the flour until well covered. If you're feeling especially crispy, first dredge through flour, then egg, and then flour again. Choice is yours.

5. By now, the pan should be toasty. Add the steaks to the oil and fry for about 4-5 minutes on each side. Add more oil as necessary, i.e., when the steak absorbs more than 50%.

6. As the steaks are done, place them on a cookie cooling rack to stay crisp.

7. Once you are done frying all of the steaks, add the coconut milk to the pan and whisk the drippings. This is the very best part!

8. To serve, top the steak with the delicious gravy.

Options/Notes:

- What is cube steak? It's usually top round or top sirloin that has been beaten within a half inch of its life give or steak a bit (see what I did there? Steak = take?)

Serves: 2 adults with leftovers

Zucchini Lasagna

Ingredients:

1-pound ground beef

1 onion

½ cup cremini mushrooms

Garlic, to taste

27 oz. can of diced tomatoes

1-2 teaspoons basil

1-2 teaspoons oregano

½ teaspoon marjoram

Salt, to taste

Ground cayenne, a pinch

2-3 zucchini

1-2 whole tomatoes sliced thinly

Parmesan cheese or vegan alternative

Tools:

Medium pan

Cutting board

Knife

Can opener

Slotted spoon or strainer

Mandolin (if you have one, otherwise use knife)

Anti-stick spray

8"x8" pan

Directions:

1. Start by browning your ground beef in medium pan on medium heat.

2. Add onion and cook for 3 minutes.

3. Add mushrooms and garlic, and cook for an additional 3 minutes.

4. Separate the diced tomatoes from the juice either using a slotted spoon or strainer and add to the pan with the spices.

5. As your sauce mixture cooks down, slice the zucchini into thin lasagna noodles. This is best done on a mandolin, but you can do this using a knife and a steady hand.

6. Cover the bottom of an 8"x8" pan with the meat sauce and arrange a layer of zucchini.

7. Repeat.

8. Cover the zucchini with the rest of the sauce if you have any left.

9. Top with the sliced tomatoes and cheese.

10. Bake at 375 for one hour.

Options/Notes:

- If you cannot handle dairy products, leave the dairy out or use a lactose free or vegan alternative.

- If you'd like something a little different, you can use eggplant instead of, or in addition to, the zucchini.

Serves: 2 adults with leftovers

VEGGIES & SIDE DISHES

Recipes included:

- Mashed Plantains
- Mashed Cauliflower
- Baked Broccoli w/ Lemon
- Sauted Spinach and Pine Nuts
- Mashed Sweet Potatoes
- Sauteed Brussels Sprouts
- Mexican Rice Style Quinoa
- Rosemary Zucchini
- Roasted Radishes
- Sauteed Swiss Chard
- Green Beans and Shallots
- Asparagus
- Cauliflower Rice
- Tomato Cucumber Salad

Mashed Plantains

Ingredients:

4 brown plantains, peeled, sliced in half lengthwise
2 tablespoons coconut oil
1 teaspoon cinnamon
Pinch of salt
2 tablespoons canned coconut milk
½ cup broth, chicken, beef, veggie (see notes)

Tools:

Cutting board
Knife
Medium pan
Measuring spoons and cup
Food processor or blender

Directions:

1. Peel your plantains by chopping the ends off and then peeling away the skin.

2. Slice in half, hot dog style.

3. Heat coconut oil on medium. When hot, add plantains and sprinkle with cinnamon and salt.

4. Cook each side for 3-5 minutes, letting it get nice and brown.

5. Remove plantains from oil and add to food processor with coconut milk. Turn it on and add your broth, ⅛ of a cup at a time until it reaches a consistency you like. Taste to see if you need more salt.

Options/Notes:

- This dish involves a little thinking ahead. Plantains should have brown skin when you prepare them. The brown indicates that they will be sweeter and easier to peel. It's the difference between an under ripe, green banana versus a bright yellow banana.

- As for what broth to put into your plantains, it really depends on what type of meat you are eating. If you are serving these with beef, use beef broth. With chicken or pork, use the chicken broth. If you don't want any meat, use the veggie. Try them all and see what YOU like best.

Serves: 2 adults

Mashed Cauliflower

Ingredients:

1 small cauliflower

3 tablespoons butter

¼-½ teaspoon powdered garlic

1-2 teaspoon parsley

Salt and pepper, to taste

½ cup broth (chicken, beef, or veggie)

Tools:

Pot with lid

Steamer basket (optional)

Cutting board

Knife

Food processor or blender

Measuring spoons and cup

Directions:

1. Fill your pot with 1-2" of water, insert steamer basket (if using), and pot lid on. Bring to a boil.

2. While you wait for the water to boil, cut your cauliflower into 1" pieces.

3. Add cauliflower to steamer basket or water, cover with lid, and steam for 7-10 minutes.

4. To tell if cauliflower is done, stab it with a fork. If the for slides in easily, it is done. If not, cover and cook for another 2 minutes, and test again after 2 minutes.

5. When cauliflower is done, strain and place in food processor with butter, garlic, parsley, salt, pepper, and ¼ cup of the broth. Add more broth as needed. Blend until smooth.

Options/Notes:

- You can also add other herbs and spices, such as Italian spices mixtures, basil, or oregano. For a bit of a cheesy flavor, add some nutritional yeast.

Serves: 2 adults

Baked Broccoli with Lemon

Ingredients:

1 bunch broccoli, roughly cut to even sized pieces
1 tablespoon coconut oil
Salt and pepper, to taste
1 lemon, sliced thinly

Tools:

Cutting board
Knife
Bowl
Measuring spoon
Spoon
Anti-stick spray
Baking sheet

Directions:

1. Preheat oven to 375 degrees.

2. Roughly chop your broccoli to roughly the same size. Think bite sized.

3. Toss in a bowl with coconut oil, salt, and pepper.

4. Spray baking sheet with anti-stick stuff, and then put broccoli on pan.

5. Thinly slice lemon, and add to the top of the broccoli.

6. Bake for 20-30 minutes. I like it when it's a little crunchy.

Options/Notes:

- If you're looking for something a little different, search your grocery stores for Romanesco broccoli. It's a neat hybrid of broccoli and cauliflower and has pointy ends (not sharp). It's a nifty looking vegetables and tastes exquisite, despite its weird appearance.

Serves: 2 adults

Sautéed Spinach and Pine Nuts

Ingredients:

¼ cup pine nuts
1-2 tablespoons cooking fat
2 cloves garlic
2-3 cups spinach
Salt and pepper, to taste

Tools:

Medium pan
Small bowl
Measuring spoons
Cutting board
Knife
Tongs

Directions:

1. Heat pan on medium high heat. This is one of the few times to heat it up with NO cooking fat.

2. Mince garlic while the pan is heating.

3. When hot, add pine nuts. Let nuts cook for about 30 seconds on each side, until they are browned.

4. Remove from heat and set aside in a small bowl.

5. Return pan to burner, and add cooking fat.

6. When melted or hot, add garlic and cook for 1-2 minutes.

7. Add spinach to pan and cook for another 1-2 minutes, stirring frequently.

8. As soon as ¼ of the spinach is bright green, turn heat off and add pine nuts. Toss to incorporate and remove from stove. Serve immediately.

Options/Notes:

- If you're looking to make this easier on yourself, buy the diced or minced garlic from the grocery store. It cuts down on time spent in the kitchen and more time doing what you love to do.

Serves: 2 adults

Mashed Sweet Potatoes

Ingredients:

2 large sweet potatoes
Salt and pepper, to taste
2 tablespoons butter

Tools:

Vegetable peeler
Cutting board
Knife
Medium pot
Fork
Measuring spoons and cup
Food processor or blender

Directions:

1. Peel the sweet potatoes.

2. Dice the potatoes to bite size pieces.

3. Place sweet potatoes in medium pot and fill with water. Make sure water is at least an inch above them.

4. Bring to a boil on medium heat and cook for 10-15 minutes. To test if the sweeties are done, use a fork and pierce one. If the fork slides through easily, the potatoes are done.

5. Reserve ½ to a cup of the water from the sweet potatoes. Drain the rest.

6. Put the sweet potatoes in food processor with butter, salt, and pepper.

7. Start to puree, adding ¼ cup of water at a time until blended smooth.

8. Taste and adjust spices and butter as you prefer.

Serves: 2 adults with leftovers

Sautéed Brussels Sprouts

Ingredients:

1 pound Brussels sprouts
1 tablespoon bacon grease
2 cloves of garlic, minced
Salt and pepper, to taste

Tools:

Cutting board
Knife
Medium pan with lid
Measuring spoons
Spatula

Directions:

1. Cut the bottoms off the Brussels sprouts and remove the outer leaves. Cut into quarters and halves to create even pieces.

2. Heat pan over medium heat.

3. Add bacon grease.

4. When grease is melted, add Brussels sprouts, garlic, salt, and pepper.

5. Sauté for 5 minutes.

6. Sauté for an additional 5 minutes with the lid on, until Brussels sprouts are tender.

Options/Notes:

- Go easy on the salt due to the bacon grease having a fair amount of salt in it.

Serves: 2 adults with leftovers

Mexican Rice Style Quinoa

Ingredients:

1 cup quinoa

3 tablespoons cooking fat

¼ cup onion, diced

½ teaspoon minced garlic

½ teaspoon salt

1 teaspoon cumin

1 cup canned diced tomatoes

1 cup chicken or veggie broth

Tools:

Colander

Large saucepan with lid

Measuring cups and spoons

Cutting board

Knife

Spatula

Directions:

1. Rinse quinoa or buy the pre-rinsed kind.

2. Heat cooking fat in large saucepan over medium heat.

3. Add quinoa. Stir constantly until quinoa starts to brown, about 2-4 minutes. You'll also start to smell a pleasant, nutty aroma.

4. Stir in onions, garlic, salt, and cumin. Cook for an additional 2-5 minutes, until onions start to turn translucent.

5. Add tomatoes and chicken broth. Bring to a boil.

6. Reduce heat to low, cover, and simmer for 20-25 minutes.

Serves: 2 adults with leftovers

Rosemary Zucchini

Ingredients:

3-4 zucchinis
Rosemary (fresh really is better with this one)
Salt and pepper to taste
1 tablespoon butter or cooking oil

Tools:

Cutting board
Knife
Medium pan
Measuring spoon

Directions:

1. Heat a medium frying pan on medium heat with a tablespoon of cooking oil/butter.

2. Slice your zucchini, discarding the ends. Slice it hotdog style and then slice into little half moons.

3. When the pan is hot, add your zucchini, add salt, pepper, and rosemary to taste and sauté until they soften a bit, about 7-8 minutes.

Roasted Radishes

Ingredients:

1 bunch of radishes

1-2 tablespoons coconut oil

1-2 teaspoons dried rosemary

Tools:

Cutting board

Knife

Measuring spoon

Baking sheet

Directions:

1.
1. Preheat oven to 375 degrees.

2. Wash radishes and chop tops off. Save them for later.

3. Half and quarter them so they are approximately the same size.

4. Toss radishes with coconut oil, and sprinkle rosemary on top.

5. Bake for 10-15 minutes.

6. While the radishes bake, chop the green tops of the radishes.

7. Add the tops to the radishes, stir, and bake for an additional 5 minutes.

Serves: 2 adults

Sautéed Swiss Chard

Ingredients:

1 tablespoon coconut oil
2 cloves garlic
1 bunch Swiss chard
½-1 lemon, juiced

Tools:

Cutting board
Knife
Medium pan
Spatula

Directions:

1. Dice garlic, or use the pre-chopped kind.

2. Heat pan on medium heat. Add coconut oil.

3. Add garlic to the pan when the coconut oil has melted.

4. Sauté for 1-2 minutes.

5. While garlic is cooking, chop the Swiss chard roughly. You can eat the stalk of this leafy green.

6. Add chard to pan and sauté until it starts to turn bright green, about 3 minutes.

7. Add lemon juice and stir.

8. Remove from heat and serve immediately.

Options/Notes:

*   Swiss chard comes in a few different varieties, white, yellow, and red. I like the red for it's beautiful color. It has wide flat leaves, and is absolutely delicious.

*   Feel free to use other greens, such as mustard greens, collard greens, or kale.

*   If you want this a little creamy, add ¼ cup of canned coconut milk when you add the lemon. It's one my husband's favorite winter side dishes.

Serves: 2 adults

Green Beans and Shallots

Ingredients:

1 pound green beans
1-2 shallots
1-2 tablespoons butter
Salt and pepper, to taste

Tools:

Medium pan with lid
Steamer basket (optional)
Cutting board
Knife
Small pan
Measuring spoons
Spatula
Colander or strainer

Directions:

1. (*Optional*) Snap the ends off your green beans and re-move the string that runs lengthwise. Depending on my timeline for the evening, I may or may not do this.

2. In the medium pan, fill with about an inch of water (or if you have a steamer basket, you can steam them that way). Cover with lid and bring to a boil.

3. Remove the peel of your shallot, chop of the ends, then slice into thin rounds.

4. When the medium pan starts to boil, add green beans and steam for 3-7 minutes. They should change to bright green. Taste to see if they're done. They should stil have a nice crunch to them.

5. Heat small pan over medium heat, add butter, and let it melt.

6. Sauté shallots for about 3 minutes, until translucent.

7. Remove green beans from heat, strain water, and douse with cold water to stop them from cooking further.

8. Top with shallots and butter.

Options/Notes:

- You can either steam the green beans in a steamer basket or in the pan with water. Either option works.

Serves: 2 adults

Lemon Asparagus

Ingredients:

1 bunch of asparagus, approximately 1 pound

Zest of one lemon

2 cloves garlic, minced

½-1 tablespoon coconut oil

Salt and pepper, to taste

Tools:

Cutting board

Knife

Zester (or a veggie peeler)

Baking sheet

Tin foil (for easy clean up)

Measuring spoon

Directions:

1. Turn broiler to high.

2. Cut about 1" off of the bottom of the asparagus. This part is usually bitter and hard to chew.

3. Zest the lemon. If you do not have a zester, use a veggie peeler to take the first layer. Try to avoid the white part of the lemon as that is bitter.

4. Line a baking sheet with tin foil (optional).

5. Place all ingredients on baking sheet and toss with coconut oil.

6. Broil for 5-7 until the tips are crispy.

Options/Notes:

• This recipe is easily modified for the grill. All you need to do is place on the grill for a couple of minutes and voila!

• Another option is to peel the bottom portion of the asparagus rather than cut. It wastes less of the stalks, and it's completely up to you.

• How to select asparagus: look for vibrant green spears that are firm. The tips should still be compact.

• WARNING: This dish may make your pee smell funny. The mister and I laugh about it when we have them.

Serves: 2 adults

Cauliflower Rice

Ingredients:

1 small cauliflower

2-4 tablespoons coconut oil or other cooking fat

Salt and pepper, to taste

Other spices (optional... specific, I know)

Tools:

Cutting board

Knife

Medium pan

Measuring spoons and cup

Spatula

Food processor with shredding disk (if you don't have this, you can always use your blender and pulse it until it looks like rice pieces).

Directions:

1. Dice your cauliflower so that it can fit into the insertion part of your food processor.

2. Shred the cauliflower. This can sometimes be a messy process. The cauliflower is pretty light and likes to fly out of the food processor. As the old Domino's commercials used to say, "You're free, cheesy bread!"

3. Heat pan on medium heat. Add cooking fat when hot. Let it melt and then add cauliflower.

4. Add salt, pepper, and any other spices you like, such as garlic and/or parsley.

5. Sauté for about 5 minutes.

Options/Notes:

- Cauli-rice is extremely versatile. You can eat it as plain rice, add spices to it to match your meal, or use it to stuff vegetables, as you would with normal rice. I also like to use it in soups to give a texture similar to rice. For Mexican food, I add a little cilantro and lime juice. Indian food gets cumin and/or curry powder, maybe event turmeric. Italian food goes great with basil or an Italian herb blend.

Serves: 2 adults

Tomato Cucumber Salad

Ingredients:

3-4 Roma tomatoes
1 small cucumber
3-6 leaves fresh basil
2 cloves garlic
¼-½ cup olive oil
⅛-¼ cup balsamic vinegar
Salt and pepper, to taste

Tools:

Cutting board
Knife
Bowl
Measuring cup
Spoon

Directions:

1. Dice tomato and add to bowl.

2. Peel cucumber (if you don't like skin), and slice lengthwise (hotdog). If it is bigger than 1" in diameter, use a spoon to scrap out the seeds (also optional). Dice cucumber and add to bowl.

3. Cut up your basil and add to bowl.

4. Add remaining ingredients, starting with the smaller quantities for each and adjust to taste.

Options/Notes:

- If making the salad early, leave it on the counter so that the flavors can blend together in the warm air. The cold air of the fridge does not allow them to mingle as much.

- Other items you can add are small mozzarella balls (bocconcini) or fresh black olives.

Serves: 2 adults

DESSERTS

Recipes included:

- Bananas Foster
- Sautéed Apples
- Strawberry Banana Ice Cream
- Chocolate Banana Nut Ice Cream

Bananas Foster

Ingredients:

6 tablespoons butter
6 ripe bananas
1 cup brown sugar or coconut sugar
Splash of canned coconut milk
⅔ cup rum
Pinch of cinnamon
Vanilla ice cream (optional, dairy or not)

Tools:

Large pan
Cutting board
Knife
Spatula
Lighter

Directions:

1. In a large pan, melt butter on medium low heat.

2. As pan is heating and butter is melting, peel your bananas. You will then stick your finger into the end of the banana, and gently push through the entire piece. This will split the bananas into thirds.

3. Cut the now third banana into 2" long pieces.

4. Add the sugar to the pan and stir until dissolved, about 2 minutes.

5. Add coconut milk.

6. Add bananas and cook for about 3 minutes or until they brown.

7. Remove from heat and add rum and a sprinkle of cinnamon.

8. Tip the pan so that it is at about a 45 -degree angle. Use a lighter and light the banana mixture on fire. Seriously, light that sucker up!

9. While the flaming bananas are going on, gently shake the pan, coating every side of them. The fire will eventually go out, once all of the alcohol is cooked out.

10. Serve over ice cream.

Options/Notes:

- One of the main reasons this dish is so fun to make is because you set it on fire. Really! How many times do you get told you get to torch a dish? This is one of those times! Have fun! And maybe **<u>DON'T</u>** make this while intoxicated. That could end very badly and my uncle the fire marshal may have to come visit your house.

Serves: 4 adults

Sautéed Apples

Ingredients:

2-3 apples, peeled and diced

3-4 tablespoons butter

Cinnamon, to taste

Nutmeg, to taste

Salt, a pinch

1-2 tablespoons honey, maple syrup, or coconut syrup

Vanilla ice cream (optional, dairy or not)

Tools:

Veggie peeler

Cutting board

Apple slicer (if you have one)

Knife

Medium pan

Measuring spoons

Directions:

1. Peel apples.

2. Using the apple slicer, slice apples, and then dice them into bite size pieces.

3. Heat pan on medium heat. Add butter.

4. When butter is melted, add apples and spices. Sauté for 5-8 minutes, until the apples start to soften.

5. Add sweetener and cook for an additional 2 minutes, stirring regularly.

Options/Notes:

• If you want to add a little bam to this, add a splash of rum. Yum!

• Serve over ice cream if you want some creamy deliciousness.

Serves: 2 adults

Strawberry Banana Ice Cream

Ingredients:

2 frozen bananas

1 cup frozen strawberries

¼-½ cup of canned coconut milk

2-4 tablespoons honey, maple syrup, or coconut syrup

Tools:

Cutting board

Knife

Food processor

Measuring cups and spoons

Directions:

1. Peel bananas, cut into ½" to 1" slices.

2. Remove tops of strawberries, and quarter them.

3. Freeze fruit for about 2 hours.

4. Add all ingredients to food processor and blend on high until smooth. You may need to add more or less coconut milk. Play with it until it has the consistency you like. It may take up to 8 minutes to blend.

Options/Notes:

- This is a light recipe that you can add as much or as little sweetener as you like. Play and have fun.

- You can also add different berries, a mixture, or whatever else you'd like.

- This recipe is best used in a food processor. The shape of the blade is more effective than a blender.

- If you ever have berries or bananas that are about to go bad, freezing them is an excellent way to save them. Slice them into the sizes you want and then freeze in plastic bags. You will then have them on hand for ice cream or smoothies.

Serves: 2 adults

Chocolate Banana Nut Ice Cream

Ingredients:

2 frozen bananas

1-2 tablespoons nut butter (almond, cashew, macadamia)

¼ cup chopped chocolate bar

¼-½ cup of canned coconut milk

2-4 tablespoons honey, maple syrup, or coconut syrup

Tools:

Cutting board

Knife

Food processor

Measuring cups and spoons

Directions:

1. Peel bananas, cut into ½" to 1" slices.

2. Freeze banana for about 2 hours.

3. Add all ingredients to food processor and blend on high until smooth. You may need to add more or less coconut milk. Play with it until it has the consistency you like. It may take up to 8 minutes to blend.

Options/Notes:

- This is a light recipe that you can add as much or as little sweetener as you like. Play and have fun.

- This recipe is best used in a food processor. The shape of the blade is more effective than a blender.

- If you ever have berries or bananas that are about to go bad, freezing them is an excellent way to save them. Slice them into the sizes you want and then freeze in plastic bags. You will then have them on hand for ice cream or smoothies.

Serves: 2 adults

DRINKS & JUICES

Recipes included:

- Sangria
- Watermelon Cucumber Juice
- Carrot Parsley Juice
- Mimosa
- Orange, Mango, Carrot Goodness

Sangria

Ingredients:

1 lemon
1 orange
1 lime
A couple of slices of pineapple
1 bottle of cabernet or merlot
Splash of pineapple juice
Splash of orange juice
2-3 tablespoons sugar or coconut sugar
Ginger ale

Tools:

Cutting board
Knife
Pitcher

Directions:

1. Slice all your fruit into wedges and squeeze juice into pitcher.

2. Put all fruit, including squeezed fruit, into pitcher.

3. Add wine, pineapple juice, orange juice, and sugar

4. Let sit overnight in the fridge.

5. Serve over ice with ginger ale.

Options/Notes:

- A great, cheap wine for this is Two Buck Chuck (Charles Shaw wine), available at Trader Joe's.

- This doesn't necessarily have to sit overnight, but it is best when it has time to incorporate.

- If you're looking for an extra kick, try adding brandy or rum. Just be careful because this stuff is delicious!

- It is also a very easy recipe to double, or even triple. How wild do you and your friends plan to get is the real question.

Serves: 4 adults

Watermelon Cucumber Juice

Ingredients:

1 cucumber
½ watermelon
Mint leaves (optional)

Tools:

Cutting board
Knife
Juicer

Directions:

1. Wash your cucumber.

2. Cut the rind (the green part of the watermelon) off.

3. Put in juicer. If using mint leaves, add them first.

Serves: 2 adults or 1 really, really thirsty adult

Carrot Parsley Juice

Ingredients:

1 bunch of parsley
6-10 carrots

Tools:
Juicer

Directions:

1. Put your parsley in the juicer first.

2. Then put the carrots in there. If the parsley is too strong tasting, add more carrot until you get something you like.

Options/Notes:

- This is super great for your digestive tract. If gives you a breath mint from the inside!

Serves: 2 adults or 1 really, really thirsty adult

Mimosa

Ingredients:

4 oranges
1 bottle of champagne

Tools:

Cutting board
Knife
Juicer

Directions:

1. Peel your orange and run it through the juicer.

2. Pour a bit of fresh juice into each glass.

3. Top off with champagne.

Options/Notes:

*   To make this a Bellini, just use peaches instead!

Serves: How rowdy does your tribal brunch get? It could serve 2 or 8. You choose!

Orange, Mango, Carrot Goodness

Ingredients:

⅛-¼ teaspoon turmeric

6-10 carrots

3-4 oranges

1 handful thawed frozen mango OR 1-2 ripe mangos

½ ginger

Tools:

Juicer

Directions:

1. Place your turmeric at the bottom of the juice catcher.

2. Juice the other ingredients.

3. Stir juice before serving.

Serves: 2 adults

THANK YOU

For most of my life, I've criticized actors and performers for their thank yous and how stupid and flustered they look when they win those awards. In no way, shape, or form is this some kind of award, but now I realize how hard thank yous are to actually put together. Who do you thank first? What if you forget that one person you met in the grocery store? There's a lot of pressure here!

First, I would like to thank both sides of my family. Thank you for celebrating everything with food, for whispering the secrets of your food to me and for letting me help with Sunday brunches after church. Thank you for teaching me that you feed a cold, you feed happiness, you feed everything. Thank you for making the dinner table a fun place to be family, whether we're yelling and screaming just to be heard in the chaos or coming together when tragedy is present.

It may seem odd, but the next person I'd like to thank is my amazing accountant Paula. I am still "blaming" you for this book. I appreciate your friendship, love, and thoroughly incredible accounting skills keeping my family on track. Warren and I are forever grateful to you. You can check out her blog at https://pdwms.wordpress.com/. She's hilarious!

Dearest Husband and our two princess kitties, thank you for believing in me, for cheering me on, meowing, and bringing me a sparkly ball to throw when I was starting to freak out. My love, thank you for reminding me about Jimi and listening to "All Along the Watchtower" on repeat so that I could focus. Without you three in my life, this process would have taken way longer and probably been more painful, and without a doubt, less interesting.

To my unborn Little Turkey, thank you for choosing me to be your mommy and getting the fire lit under my ass so that when you come into this world, Mommy and Daddy can actually spend time with you, not worrying about getting a book done, getting to know you and teaching you how to be human the best way we know how. No promises that you'll be very human given Mom's a monkey and Dad's a fish.

Thank you, Evelina, for dealing with my crazy breakdowns, for the "I just can't," the "I'm so stupid for even thinking I can do this," and "The sun is refusing to shine." Thank you for giving me permission to grieve and not work when we lost Nana Mary and Little Bird. Truly, I could not have done this without you and your constant support. Thank you.

My inspiring Black Cats, wonderful Tribal Sisters, my coaches, both personal and professional, my Mountain Sisters, my Alchemist Sisters, my Desert Sage Sisters, and the sisters I have yet to meet, thank you for being the reason this came together. Without knowing you, I wouldn't have had the audacity to even attempt to write this or bring women together. Thank you for your laughter, support, the wine, and the never-ending, "When's the book coming out?!" I am honored to be amongst you and part of your world.

And last but not least, you, my dearest readers! Thank you for coming to this space and exploring! I hope you have some creative juices flowing and are gearing up to start your own Tribal Brunch. The world needs you out there reaching out to create community!

Blessed be,
Kirsten D'Agostaro Shook

Proof

Made in the USA
Charleston, SC
12 September 2016